il teatro dei SAPORI

Guelfo Magrini

Brunello
di Montalcino

morg
anti
editori

summary

1. An itinerary with Brunello 8

2. The territory 20

3. The history of Brunello 30

4. Under the sign of Sangiovese 52

5. From vineyard to cellar 62

6. The other wines of Montalcino 98

7. The land of Brunello 118

8. Typical products and cuisine 150

9. Museum and folklore 196

10. The producers 206

A gastronomical tour of the land of Brunello 274

Bibliography 280

Contents 283

A wine
of success

Brunello di Montalcino is now considered one of the most important wines in the world. what factors have contributed to attaining such excellence?

I

1 - vineyard in Castel Giocondo

2 - vine with bunches of Sangiovese grapes

A wine of success

3 - tasting Brunello

More than character, it is a sum of qualities that makes the difference, distinguishing Brunello di Montalcino from other red d.o.c.g. wines from Tuscany and the many 'vermigli' produced in the world. Brunello is not the result of a synergy between various enological components, which is what happens with the Bordeaux 'assemblies', for example, or the mixing of different vinifications between Cabernet Sauvignon, Merlot and Cabernet franc, carefully selected by the producers along the variegated Acquitan coast, following various and repeated tasting.

Neither is it a wedding between different species of vines, formulated and mixed, choosing the best of the historical territorial production, as demonstrated in the recipe of Baron Ricasoli, the inventor of Chianti, a wine that is a balanced composition between 'the magnificent four' local vines (Sangiovese, Canaiolo, Trebbiano and Colorino), and which was for decades the very emblem of Italian wine.

Brunello instead is the result of the masterful vinification of a single vine, Sangiovese, which has amply demonstrated its natural disposition for an alliance with the territory of Montalcino.

It is a land caressed by the sun, with the characteristic shape of cypress trees, recorded time and again in the most beautiful landscape photos of Tuscany; a laborious and happy land, attentive to tradition, but open to new and interesting developments occurring in the surrounding area. It is a spontaneous, rough land, determined to earn respect, especially for its ability to produce rich, balanced and healthy clusters of the best grapes.

Thanks to the individual and collective intelligence of Tuscany's large and small winegrowers, its institutional representatives and the many creative personalities who accompany its winning image, undeniably prestigious results have been attained, through research for the constant and ubiquitous application of standards of agronomical, enological and commercial excellence. So the fame of Brunello goes beyond the mere quality of its grapes. It involves the geo-pedological conformation of the territory and its climactic component, which are represented in the work of the producers, who observe a few simple formulas: good

4 - leaves of the Colorino vine

5 - bottle of Brunello di Montalcino with the docg collar

6 - barrique cellar

7 - ancient tool once
used to cork bottles

8 - cask rings ➡

land, good air, a little blessed water, a lot of sun and a great commitment. Another of the peculiarities that make this wine great is the difference of style expressed by individual vineyards, albeit they all follow a common fil rouge.

There are a little over two hundred winegrowers who produce Brunello, distributed over the 1.400 hectares of vineyards enrolled in the registry. During the most recent vintages, more than five million bottles have been produced, of which about a fifth is for Reserve. Just to make a single comparison, the area of the nearby Chianti d.o.c.g. area amounts to 23 thousand hectares, distributed among 7.000 producers.

Even the area of the vineyards enrolled in the Brunello registry has grown, from a few score

9 - harvest

hectares of a decade or so ago to the 1,400 hectares of today. At present, among the other d.o.c.g. areas and denominations produced in the territory of Montalcino (Red, Moscadello, Sant'Antimo and Sienese Hills Chianti) more than 2.500 hectares of vineyards can be counted, distributed throughout a municipal territory of 24 thousand hectares. We can also speak of genius loci for Brunello, as it is capable and has been so for only a few years, of guaranteeing the widespread prosperity that was unknown in the not too distant past. Just think that Montalcino wines today produce a turnover of 200 billion lire, providing 800 full-time jobs and employment for 600 temporary workers.

More than half of the Ilcinese winegrowers occupy an area of less than three hectares, dimensions that are not at all distant from reference figures for the national winegrowing sector.

10 - aging bottles in the cellar

More in detail, 22 percent of the winegrowers have an area dedicated to vines of less than 1 hectare; 29 percent own between 1 and 3 hectares; 15 percent between 3 and 5 hectares, 15 percent between 5 and 15 hectares, 9 percent between 15 and 100 hectares, 1 percent over 100 hectares and the remaining 9 percent indicates exclusively commercial firms.

Vineyard management in Montalcino is another factor to be taken into consideration, inasmuch as it assumes a peculiar aspect due to the variegated social composition of workers in the division.

There are first of all the historical producers: the landowning families, whose surnames have been in the city population registry for generations, including the very 'inventors' of Brunello. Alongside them are cultivators who have planted

11 - Montalcino, panorama

vineyards in old land holdings inherited from their families' past condition as sharecroppers, together with expert vineyard farmers or enologists from other winegrowing regions. A widespread phenomenon is the presence of new entrepreneurs, who have come to these hills from various European cities on the returning wave of re-immigration to rural areas in the seventies. It is in this environment that the friendly and fertile enological confrontation takes place between simple enthusiasts, artists, professional people and managers, previously dedicated to other industrial or artisan craft divisions, who have found here a dimension more suitable to their creative inspiration or existential desires.

The success of Brunello also derives from a continuous research to ensure the supremacy of the image over the wine's direct competitors, the prestigious red wines and the wine cellars of the world.

For this reason, Brunello has increasingly enjoyed more widespread international appraise, since a good 64 out of every 100 bottles are sold abroad, in countries where the competition of wines from other winegrowing areas of the world is particularly stiff. The countries that seek and import Brunello most assiduously and faithfully are Germany, Switzerland, the United States, Japan, Canada and England.

In this wine, which reflects the greatness of this docg area and makes the Sienese land even more precious, this mixture of hope, dedication and competence, the personal or family experience of so many heterogeneous and apparently distant personalities, has created an amalgamation that cannot be found elsewhere.

12 - the historical wine cellars ➡ of the Ciacci Piccolomini d'Aragona vineyard

13 - wine cellar tools

The territory

The initial approach to the land
of Brunello is with its complex and
fascinating geology, the hills, the
water and the changes brought about
by man through the centuries

14 - cypress trees
between Torrenieri and
San Quirico d'Orcia

15 - Montalcino, roofs

The territory

Montalcino is the centre of what was once Etruria, as shown on the archaeological maps that indicate the primary settlements of the ancient italic civilisation. The mass of hills whose eastern balcony is
home to its inhabited centre is extremely wide and
easily defensible from the point of view of ancient
colonies, dominating as it does the surrounding
16 - poppy fields   area for kilometres in all directions. The area is arti-

culated among high hills, low, fertile plains and narrow valleys, down to the banks of the most important rivers of the Sienese province.

It is reminiscent of a square, whose sides measure an average of 15 kilometres and are lapped by the waters of four different courses of water.

The largest and most important is the Ombrone, a capricious and authoritative river, despite the modest dimensions of its riverbed. The Ombrone washes the buttresses of the Alcinese territory to the northwest. It meets the unpredictable Arbia creek, which flows north for a short distance and then turns east, giving its name to a wide, sinuous and low valley, which already had two intercity highways crossing it during ancient times: the Cassian road, of the ancient Roman period, and the Francigena road, which is a more recent tract that dates from late medieval times, used prevalently for religious pilgrimages. The two roads follow the valley for a long tract, joining at Borgo Torrenieri and continuing in the direction of the capital.

The eastern side of the Montalcino quadrilateral meets the Asso creek, while on the south, the Orcia River flows through its valley, with numerous castles perched on the summits of the barren and rough

17 - the Orcia River

foothills before the slopes of Mount Amiata. The mountain, which dominates the south, is an authoritative volcanic mass that still shows signs of its glorious eruptive past, through the numerous thermal fountains that spring from its slopes. It is the mountain that dominates the Brunello territory and which guarantees protection from the scirocco tempests coming from the south. On quiet days, one can see the Tyrrhenian Sea in the far-off distance, along with the Lazio mountains and the tranquil waters of Lake Trasimeno and Lake Bolsena. It is a clear-cut, strong profile that emerges from the vast range of the sweet Alcinese hills.

Montalcino is located about 40 kilometres south of Siena. Its territory is articulated over an area of 243.62 square kilometres (of which 29 percent is plains, 70 percent hills and 1 percent mountain) and is the most extensive territory in the Sienese province. Agriculture is specialised mainly in olive groves (8 percent) and obviously, winegrowing, with 11 percent of the cultivated land area occupied (of which 55 percent is enrolled in the Brunello registry).

The agricultural and therefore economic panorama thus concludes with 36 percent of the territory given over to sowable crops, pastures and other crops, including orchards, with a prevalence of plums, which assume increasingly greater importance for the valley portions of the Ombrone.

The Montalcino hill is 40 km from the sea as the crow flies (and it was covered with that sea millions of years ago) and, to the west, which looks onto the Grossetto Maremma, the inco-

18 - new vineyard plantation, with Mt. Amiata in the background

19 and 20 - pruning and tying the vines

21 - Sant'Angelo Scalo, ➡
a field of grain with rainbow

ming marine winds can be felt to a great extent, lowering the average summer temperatures and raising winter temperatures.

The characteristics of the soil are extremely diversified, due to both its make up and structure: the lower areas are made up of terrain originating from the deposit of detritus, with a deep active quaternary layer, which is quite loose. Overlaying this, the terrain is enriched with skeletal elements, while the active layer is reduced, determining soils formed from the decomposition of the original rocks, especially clay and albite.

The terrains present an average clay content, rich in limestone, mixed with large areas of tuff, which tend to be lean. Just a few hundred metres from each other, therefore, areas rich in limestone split with clay and albite coexist with vast portions of terrain with a greater clay content and fewer skeletal elements and areas made up of terrain formed from the influx of alluvial detritus, according to the variations in altitude from the mouth to the head of the valley.

The climate is typically Mediterranean, with precipitation concentrated in the spring and autumn months (with an annual average of 700 mm). In winter snow above the

22 and 23 - terrains suitable for the cultivation of vines in Montalcino: with argillaceous shale, veins of clay, sandstone and riverbed rocks

altitude of 400 m is not infrequent. The proximity of mount Amiata, 1.734 m high, guarantees a natural protection against climactic events of exaggerated intensity, such as rainstorms or hail. The hillside areas, where most of the vineyards are located, rarely experience fog, freezing or late frost, while the frequent winds guarantee optimum conditions for the state of health of the vines, mitigating any insurgence of fungus pathologies.

The climate is prevalently mild, with a great number of sunny days, which ensures the gradual and complete maturation of the fruit. The presence in the territory of hillsides oriented differently, the marked modulation of the hills and the differences in altitude between the valley areas and the higher terrains (Poggio della Vivitella – 661 m asl – located in the central area of the municipal territory) determines the cohabitance of climatic micro-environments that are very different from each other, which is a factor that contributes to the great difference between one Brunello and another, albeit they are produced in nearby areas.

24 - balls of *Cotoneaster*

25 - genista

TYPICAL MONTALCINO FLORA

the flora that characterises the surrounding Montalcino area is more than ever varied and colourful, influenced by the numerous micro-climates that are present there

26 - strawberry trees

27 - mastic trees

28 - iris

29 - ficodindia

30 - wild rose

31, 32 and 33 - badger,
hares, field mice

34 and 35 - wild boar
and partridge

Concerning the vegetation, it must be said that the forest surrounding Montalcino is large and well cared for. It forms an extremely long covering of greenery that descends obliquely towards the sea. Various types of trees and shrubs make up this mosaic of vegetation; holms and other species of oak dominate the territory, surrounded by or mixed with chestnuts and manna ash, arbutus berries, lentisks and, in lower areas, bramble rose, genista, myrtle and juniper, and finally the intense officinal perfumes of a flora accustomed to rare precipitation. In the interesting array of local fauna, numerous families of hedgehogs, badgers, porcupines, beech martens, weasels and wolves move through wide natural corridors, favoured by the vast extension of the woods and greenery surrounding the Brunello vineyards, while the evening and night sky is animated by the occasionally disquieting calls of owls, owlets, barn owls and tawny owls; on days when the weather is fine it is not uncommon to sight a buzzard, a predatory bird of the falcon family that looks like a small eagle and flies majestically at impressive altitudes, or perches on electricity lines or vineyard rows, waiting for its favourite prey: rabbits or hares, frogs, field mice and at times, pheasant or partridge nests. The harrier eagle, hen harrier, windhover, the nuthatch, green woodpecker, imperial crow, wryneck and sparrow are more rare but are also present at times.

One of the emblems of the territory, the thrush, which has been hunted with no regulations of good ecological sense, has now almost disappeared. Since it is a solitary bird, the thrush suffers from the prohibitive conditions inflicted by hunting much more than does the starling. Distantly related to the nobler thrush, the starling is organised in vast flocks and defends itself much better from the snares of man; the birds organise veritable shifts of guard and observation duty to defend the group. Getting our feet back on the ground, among the animals that roam the territory, we also – and above all – find the wild boar, which is also hunted with traditional hunting parties that are today organised and controlled to guarantee the survival of the species.

36, 37, 38, 39 and 40 - buzzard, pheasants, raven, owl and owlet

The history of brunello

A trip through time to discover
how the customs, rites and history
of enological civilisation influenced
and continue to influence the
character of the wine

3

41 - the holm-oak
is the symbol of Montalcino

42 - archeological diggings
in Poggio della Civitella

The history of Brunello

43 - Etruscan funeral urn
discovered during demolition
work in Montalcino

FROM THE ORIGINS TO THE MIDDLE AGES

The industriousness of the inhabitants of the territory of Montalcino is neither new nor recent. Archaeological research carried out locally starting in the fifties revealed the presence of prehistoric settlements that were fairly large in size. On a terrace overlooking the Ombrone River valley, testimony of a prolonged 'industrial' lithic activity came to light; a veritable 'factory' of stone tools, processed with percussion methods, where over 2,000 pieces belonging to various prehistoric ages were recovered. In the surrounding areas, within a radius of 15 kilometres, Neolithic-type settlements have come to light – simple burial grounds of agricultural villages, or better organised sites in the form of circular castles, such as the ones in Poggio Civitella, Poggio Castellari or Poggio dell'Arna. The latter two were also equipped with military-type megalithic-style defensive structures.

The populations of these centres contributed to the birth of the new Etruscan civilisation, of which this land is dense with testimony and memories. Scientific research conducted in the nineties on the DNA of the population in these areas identified the greatest number of Estruscan genes extant in Italy in the present-day inhabitants of the village of Murlo, a few kilometres north of Montalcino.

Starting from the II century B.C. on the other hand, the area was overtaken by Roman expansion. The Romans were very sensitive to the attraction of pleasant and productive areas. With their organisation based on roadway communications and the rational exploitation of agriculture and forestry, they changed the face of the lands surrounding Montalcino through a system of farms for agricultural production to be marketed in the cities. Many traces of a Roman settlement of the imperial age have come to light in the current inhabited centre of Montalcino, in the locality of Santa Margherita. Various handmade goods, statues, construction stones, marbles and earthenware of Roman origin have been found almost everywhere within the city limits: a fragment of sculpture, perhaps a piece of a Roman sarcophagus, depicting a person with a cornucopia, was already inserted in the external wall during the construction of the Church of Saint Antimo, in the suburb of Castelnuovo Abate. Among the remains strewn around the abbacy buildings, the drums of temple columns can still be seen.

The decline in the economic power and prosperity created by the Roman empire was felt especially at the beginning

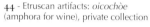

44 - Etruscan artifacts: *oicochòe* (amphora for wine), private collection

45 and 46 - Etruscan vase

47 - vineyard in Borgo a Tolli

48 - 'Blessing of the Grapes', 15th century miniature in *Missale Romanorum*, parchment code, Siena, Intronati Library

of the middle ages, in decentralised areas such as this, hard to reach and distant from the cities, which were also increasingly isolated due to continuous invasions and wars.

Life became difficult for the rural population. The countryside emptied and misery was widespread, alleviated by colonies built up around the abbacies and the contribution towards rebirth made by the friars who inhabited them.

The values and technologies that had guaranteed expression of the moderate Etruscan-Roman splendour were lost during this period, but the lines of communication remained open, less frequented by Roman patricians on vacation and more by pilgrims, seasonal workers and agricultural labourers.

From the rural documentation conserved at the duty toll stations or layovers in the area, evidence shows that for a period of many centuries, tens of thousands of sheep, directed towards the Maremma pastures, transited the tract of road from Castiglione d'Orcia to Montalcino every year, coming mostly from the Casentino area, the wide Apennine range from the provinces of Florence and Arezzo. Additionally, from the sunny, but cold and unproductive Siennese Crete areas, many people went to the Maremma to harvest grain, which matured about a month earlier there. The workers' diet, at the discretion of the occasional employer, generally included a glass of wine per day, made up of two parts wine and one part water.

In the meantime the population of Montalcino dedicated themselves to various economic activities, all of which were oriented towards nature, and the increasing cultivation of vines was not the least of them. Work in the thick woods that surround the villages has always been important in these areas. The toponym Montalcino, in fact, is derived precisely from the term '*mons ilcinus*', which in Latin means 'the mountain of holm-oaks'.

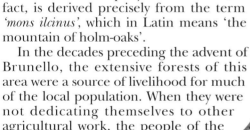

49 - Ceramic Madonna, which was hung between the rows of the vineyard to protect the harvest

In the decades preceding the advent of Brunello, the extensive forests of this area were a source of livelihood for much of the local population. When they were not dedicating themselves to other agricultural work, the people of the region would seasonally frequent the woods, sometimes moving into makeshift huts to complete the cutting of the wood, to be used whole or transformed into vegetable carbon for easier transportation to distant locations.

In areas at higher altitudes, there were small installations for the production of chestnut flour, and even the gathering of mushrooms, albeit with the prudence suggested at the time by the scarce knowledge on the subject, emerged from time

50 - topping off of the charcoal pit with clods of earth, dry leaves and soil

51 - the name of Montalcino is derived from the holm-oak (*mons ilcinus*)

to time among the archaic productive activities in the area. And the wood, or the vast forested area that it covered – now almost entirely substituted by vines – was home to every type of wildlife: storm-cocks, thrushes, wild doves and woodcocks, as well as wild boars, which were everywhere, and a few deer. It was an ideal environment to go hunting in, which is today reduced to organised teams for the hunting of wild boar.

TOWARDS BRUNELLO

The fame of these localities with respect to the immediately surrounding area is due to the many vestiges of a past in which wine is a 'fil rouge' (by name and fact) through the centuries. Enological activity definitively assumed a predominant role in the local economy only in recent decades, but its presence has always been testified to. The history of 'vermiglio' of Montalcino, which was later transformed into Brunello at the beginning of the XIX century, can be reconstructed starting from the year one thousand, thanks to the accurate chronicles and annals of local religious communities.

Throughout the long initial centuries of the second millennium, in the numerous abbacies of the area, friars favoured and diffused the cultivation of vines and the product was shared with farmers. Documentation in fact shows that the question of purchasing new vats was the order of the day, as was the sale of vineyards. The close ties between wine and this territory and its political and religious structures is also evident at the abbacy of Saint Antimo: the crypt hollowed under the main altar, a place generally utilised elsewhere for relics or ossuaries, is dedicated here to a tiny cellar for the wine used for mass, which in all probability, as the

52 - Giovannino de' Grassi and school, *'Preparation of the Casks'*, a miniature from the *Theatrum sanitatis*, second half of the 14th century, parchment code, Rome, Casanatense Library

53 - Castelnuovo dell'Abate, the Sant'Antimo Abbacy

54 - Montalcino, via Nuova

55 - Sienese lira with representing
the protagonists of he famous Palio

partly faded ancient inscriptions demonstrate, was Moscadello, the Ilcinese wine par excellence.

In the archives of the Municipality of Montalcino, transactions involving vineyards are recorded starting from the year 1200. In addition to the dates and circulation of different currencies (such as the lira, the florin, the denaro and the soldo) the toponyms of the precise localities where the vine was

grown in the vicinity are of particular interest. Some of them are still today the sites of more or less renowned wine growers.

56 - Montalcino, panorama

Reference is made to two types of real estate purchases in the detailed economic chronicles of the time. The first refers to portions of 'terrain planted with vines' in locations that are still identifiable today; in 1300, Collemattoni was already spoken of, as well as Mercato Nuovo, Poggio Lupaia, Pian dell'oro and many others. The second type of transaction, indicated with the term 'vineyard', defines parcels situated around the principle centres of the area, such as Colle, Pescaia, Villa Frassini, Contrada Conchi, Campo il Fornello and many other localities that had already been frequented since 1200.

It is impossible to identify the size of this real estate from the documents examined, but the ir-

refutable testimony of the influence of vineyards throughout the agricultural territory around the local capital is of great importance. The difference in cadastral indications between terrain planted with vines and vineyards, may possibly be explained by the methods of cultivation that were used at the time.

It is definitely known that the only unified vineyards, which were obviously of small family size, were almost always planted around the

57 - Montalcino, Medicean coat of arms placed on the fortress

58 - old wine press

areas of residence and regarded another product that qualifies the area of Montalcino: Moscadello, a sweet and corroborating wine that has been a privileged element in the diet of the Ilcinese population since ancient times.

Other vineyards, which were not of Moscadello, were promiscuously cultivated in rows with other cultivations. It can be concluded that these sparse rows, which justified denominating the terrain as being planted with vines,

were planted with red vines, from which the 'vermiglio' recalled in history was obtained. Could this
have been, perhaps, the ancestor of the Sangiovese
vine, which took the place of Moscadello in these
lands, starting from the mid 1800s?

In 1676 and 1677, Grand Duke Leopoldo II
charged senator Bartolomeo Gherardini with the

task of ascertaining the condition of the countryside in the state of Sienna. From the details and
data in his report, it appears that considerable
quantities of wine were produced in the area of
Montalcino. Of the territory in Montalcino under
cultivation, 12,5% was organised as vineyards,
while 10% of the area bordering with Buonconvento was given over to vineyards. In the area of
Buonconvento, 9.134 'some' (a system of measurement) of wine where produced. In the municipality of Montalcino, the 4.200 'some' of the capital
were added to those of the suburbs and principle
castles: 500 in Castelnuovo Abate, 700 in Sant'Angelo, 100 in Argiano and 250 in Poggio alle Mura,
for a total of 5.750 'some'. Nevertheless, it must be
noted that at the time the lands administered by
Buonconvento included vineyards that are today
part of the municipality of Montalcino. So a lot

59 - old ceramic lids utilised
in the 19th century to close
wine bottles

60 - Montalcino, Arturo Luciani. Civic and Diocese Museum of Sacred Art, 'Vaccinations in the Sienese Countryside', 1948

more wine was produced in this area than in the surrounding territory. Historical records contain many citations on the wine produced in this small area of Southern Tuscany. The marked vocation for the production of fine wines has been a well-known characteristic of the area for centuries.

In 1550 the Bolognese friar Leandro Alberti, in his *Descrittione di tutta Italia*, stated that Montalcino was "*renowned for the fine wines produced from those pleasant hills*". During a siege in 1553, the Marshall of Montluc, Commander of the Siennese garrison, stated, "*we made our faces red with the robust vermiglio wine*". Later, Pope Clemente VII, of the Medici family, said: "*they made mountain soups in the season of ripe figs, and drank a fine wine with it, which they said was greatly nutritious for the aged*".

In the 17th century many chronicles and travellers' records speak of Montalcino wine: Dutchman Francesco Scoto mentions "*Montalcino, celebrated for its Moscadello wines*" in his famous guide *Itinera Italiae*, the most widely used travellers' guide of the time, and around the end of the century, we are informed through the correspondence between Consul Sir Lambert Blackwell and the Right Noble and Honourable Blathwayt, Secretary of State at the English Court, that King William III of England drank the best Montalcino wines.

BIONDI SANTI AND BRUNELLO

The first version of one of the enological intuitions of the century was born at the Greppo Estate of Franco Biondi Santi, grandson of Ferruccio, the tenacious defender of the original recipe of Brunello wine. The story of Brunello del Greppo begins with Clemente Santi in the mid-1800s. He held a degree in pharmacy from the University of Pisa and was a scholar of nature and the territory (he carried out the first studies on the cutting of cork and on fossil bone meal, on the typical aspects of Montalcinese oleasters, the cultivation of saffron and anise). He owned a large estate between Montalcino and Pienza, and was dedicated prevalently to the reorganisation of agriculture on his land.

After reaching the oldest recognition for which there is testimony, for his Brunello, which was called 'choice red wine of 1865', he received the 'Moscatello' award at the international ex-

61 - Franco Biondi Santi

position in Paris in 1867. Clemente Santi had become a passionate enologist, and had already autonomously identified more advanced techniques of decanting and aging, with respect to the methods used at the time. In the following years, other Montalcino producers obtained important diplomas thanks to wines called 'Brunello', but among these, almost nobody was able to provide continuity in their enological experimentation, beyond the end of the First World War. Clemente Santi's daughter, Caterina, married Jacopo Biondi, a Florentine physician. Their son Ferruccio inherited the passion for wines and vine growing that had inspired his maternal grandfather, and developed even more severe standards for production in the family firm. He overcame the enormous adversities that struck European vineyards during the last century (oidium (vine mildew), peronospora and phylloxera (vine louse), with great farsightedness, remaining tenaciously attached to his idea of wine aged for long periods, with strong tannins, while Italian wine growers were increasingly oriented towards red wines for quick consumption, often 'treated', or 'enlivened' by re-fermentation provoked by the addition of slightly dried musted grapes to amplify the freshness and lightness of the final product and obtain rapid financial profits from the new vineyards planted in the American style.

He started a counter trend, through methodical clonal selection of Sangiovese, which he then re-planted in his vineyards with buds from the best parent plants identified at Greppo. He limited production to obtain grapes with richer body, extracts and acidity, selecting the best bunches, a practice that became more widespread only several decades later. The first great year for Brunello del Greppo was 1888, followed by 1891, which was equally important.

62 - lines of vines

Ferruccio's son, Trancredi, who was born in 1893, learned the secrets of the vineyard and wine cellars of the family estate from his father even before he went to earn his specialisation in the prestigious Conegliano School of Enology.

Upon the death of his father, in 1917, he remained alone in managing the Greppo Estate. He continued the work of his predecessors, but added another element to the legend of Brunello: the refilling of old Reserves. He periodically inspected all of the bottles conserved in the historic wine cellars, identifying those whose level was diminishing: he uncorked them, checked the quality of the wine contents, refilled them with wine of the same year

63 - corkscrews of every description

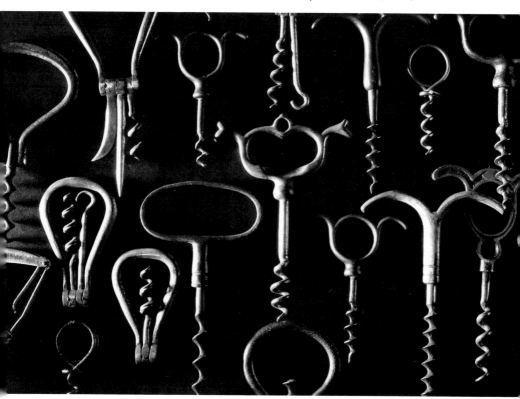

and then re-corked them. This 'rite' was celebrated for the first time in 1927, for the 1888 and 1891 Reserves. Finally, Franco Biondi Santi took over the management of the firm after earning his degree in Agricultural Sciences at the University of Perugia. He had specialised in enology and therefore set out to improve the potential of his Brunello of Montalcino, by carefully studying the various phases of vinification and aging in casks. He also collected a great selection of extraordinary year and vineyard Reserves of over 25 years of age, to enable him to attain a quality equal to the great Reserves produced by his ancestors, which had by then reached over one hundred years of age, given the continuity of the raw materials and terrain.

FROM THE FLASK TO THE BORDEAUX BOTTLE

Although the cutting edge in the initial phases along the path of this wine can be identified in the figure of Ferruccio Biondi Santi and his direct descendents, experience suggests that the official birth of Brunello di Montalcino was the fruit of the intuition of a passionate nobleman and the synergy of various local families of wine growers, involved in various capacities in the agronomic and enological definition of the new 'creature'. Research and scientific studies on wines and grapes and experiments on systems of vinification were begun in the mid-19th century by Clemente Santi, Giuseppe Anghirelli, Tito Costanti and Camillo Galassi, but the Colombine, Paccagnini and Padelletti families must also be remembered for their efforts. They were

64 - young vine leaves

65 - diploma attesting to the presence of a Brunello in 1910

among the leaders in presenting the original formula of the product on the market in the mid-1800s: pure Sangiovese grosso, an 'untreated' wine, aged for long periods in wooden casks and bottled, no longer in flasks, but in bordeaux-style bottles.

Thus, Brunello was created from Sangiovese, a veritable revolution in the culture of Italian wine; a strong and velvety wine that had characteristics that were very different from other more or less renowned aged red wines, which had in all probability taken its name from an ancient acclimatized clone of the Brunelletto vine, of which several specimens were recently recovered and conserved.

As we said earlier, the oldest bottles that have remained intact are dated 1888 and are conserved in the cellars of the Greppo Estate, owned by Biondi Santi, but the proposal of a future denomination had appeared almost a century earlier, in 1790, when Count Pieri wrote, "*a wine of only Sangiovese di Montalcino, aged in bottles for four or five years*".

The extension of the vineyards reached 925 hectares of specialised cultivation in 1929, and

66 - old winepress

1,243 hectares of mixed cultivation. These were the yeas when Brunello was starting to become well-known and was gathering consensus and awards throughout the world. This initial historic phase terminated in the thirties, when phylloxera destroyed almost all Italian vineyards. The first signs of recovery were seen as early as 1932.

67 - vine trunk in winter

68 - Montalcinese ceramic pitcher, 13th century, private collection

Montalcino gained legislative recognition: in fact, only wine produced and bottled in the municipality of Montalcino can be called Brunello. The area had already been designated in 1932 by the Ministry of Agriculture Commission.

In the fifties, local wine growers began realising the great potential of Brunello of Montalcino. The growth of consensus and image continued until 1963, when the law on 'doc' wines was passed (n° 930 of 12 July 1963). In the sixties and seventies, Brunello became increasingly famous, reaching markets throughout the world. This is the period when production and the number of producers increased. They founded a Consortium of Brunello di Montalcino on 18 April 1967, for the purpose of protecting and safeguarding the production and extending the knowledge and consumption of Brunello in Italy and throughout the world.

Thanks to Brunello and other wines, Montalcino has become one of the most visited territories for enological tourism in the world, and the many wine cellars in the area distribute as much as 19% of the wine produced locally.

69 - Banfi wine cellar for aging

70 - barrique

On 1 July 1980, Brunello of Montalcino was the first Italian wine to receive the 'docg'. It is produced exclusively from grapes of the vine that bears the same name (a selected clone of the Sangiovese grosso variety) according to regulations that limit the area of production exclusively to the municipality of Montalcino, with a maximum production of 8,000 kilos of grapes per hectare, a minimum alcohol content of 12.5, an obligatory period of aging of four years, of which three years must be in wooden casks and it must be bottled within the territorial limits. The most widespread form of vine growing in Montalcino vineyards is the spurred chord system, obtained through short pruning (with two buds) of a variable number of bunches per stalk.

Today the Brunello district has a turnover of 120 million euro in the wine business, in addition to 68 million of induced turnover from tourism and the tertiary sectors, thanks to the 900 thousand tourists that come to Montalcino annually. According to real estate market research recently conducted by the National Institute of Agricultural Economics, Brunello is at the top of the classification in determining the value of land. In this area, a hectare of vineyard has a value from 100 to 200% greater than land planted with vines with a generic indication in any other location.

According to an educated study by the University of Milan that has been carried out by researchers, if Montalcino were transformed into a new company trademark, it would value more than 500 billion lire on the open market. Recently, Brunello wine has been included in the category of 'refuge goods' and it has been considered a fine and valued investment.

under the sign of sangiovese

Brunello di Montalcino is identified
with sangiovese, a vine that has
maintained a distinctive individual
organoleptic character, despite the
extended network of genetically related
vines throughout the world

4

71 - 'pride' and Sangiovese

72 - bunches of Sangiovese grapes

under the sign of Sangiovese

73 - cork screw

The great works of art of Sangiovese, which is the name of a vine, but could very well be the 'nom de plume' of a master painter of Renaissance Tuscany, alongside Ghirlandaio, Lorenzetti and Beato Angelico, are revealed when you taste Montalcino Brunello wine and, in savouring it together with

the right dishes, you also discover its younger brother, Red.

One of the secrets of Brunello is therefore the vine, a clone of the truly numerous family of Sangiovese, which in Tuscany is still by far the most important vine grown, with almost twenty thousand hectares occupied, some 60.84% of the total, which makes it more common than any other ampelographic presence of a different genetic derivation in the area.

74 and 75 - vines in flower

In the regional panorama, it is present in almost every denomination of origin, in grape selections with other local and foreign vines, and can often be found pure in various vineyard wines, which is today a category that is almost entirely regulated by the typical geographical indications system (TGI). On the national level, it is cultivated in the central-northern areas of the country: in Umbria, it contributes to

quality wines in the Torgiano and Montefalco areas; in the Marche, it makes up the ampelographic basis of Rosso Piceno and Rosso Conero doc wines; in Romagna it is a leading vine of regional production, produced until recently in great quanitites, and vinified today with increasing care.

Sangiovese has been introduced abroad by the many Italian emigrants who have moved to vine-growing areas in the old and new worlds. Colonists from Pisa brought the vine with them and acclimatised it on the island of Corsica as early as 1400, giving it the name of Nieluccio, an extremely widespread vine today, especially in the northern part of the French island. In South America it is cultivated in Argentina, and in North America it is highly appraised in California, where it is increasingly more widespread with each passing year. Research on the ampelographic determination of this vine shows an initial exhaustive classification as early as the beginning of the 20th century, but indications of its strong personality can be found much earlier – in 1590, for example, by the erudite Solderini, in his treatise on the cultivation of vines.

76 - a bunch of Sangiovese grapes in a nineteenth century ampelographic drawing

The variety of the population of 'The Blood of Jove' is quite irregular, with biotypes that are distinguished by the size or shape of the bunch, the dimensions of the grapes, the shape of the leaves or the vigorousness of the vine.

In the territory of Montalcino, it has found expression in a genetic sequence that has enlarged the grapes and made them more sparse, and the name has been changed to Sangiovese grosso, or Brunello. In the immediate vicinity, it may also be called Prugnolo gentile, Morellino or Sangioveto, demonstrating the vine's great adaptability to the territory chosen for cultivation.

Eighty-six percent of the vineyards dedicated to the cultivation of Sangiovese were planted in the sixties, as part of the national and regional pro-

77 - a bunch
of Sangiovese grapes

grammes to launch the qualitative conversion of
vineyards. Since the eighties, thanks to contributions from the most important Tuscan universities,
research campaigns and vine shoot growing and selection operations of selected clones have produced
re-planting material that is increasingly oriented towards the traits of resistance to pathologies and vigorousness of the vine, with the production of smaller bunches and grapes of different weights.

In general, Sangiovese presents the traits of a vig-
orous vine with average germination, having robust
vines with internodes of average length. It suffers to
a small degree from chlorosis, and has a preference
for terrains that are not fertile, where it produces
grapes of good quality; it requires dry climates tending to warm, to guarantee appropriate maturation
of the grapes. It adapts well to the different growing
methods, where both short and long pruning is
used. The vines are easy to train, but require green
pruning to avoid cryptogams attacking the bunches.

The production of grapes is always constant and
abundant, but the load of buds must not be excessive, to avoid banalizing the enological potential,

78 - freshly harvested
Sangiovese grapes

the expression of which, in any case, is tied to the great care utilised in all agricultural and wine-making phases. The vine produces a harmonious, tannic wine that is of an intense ruby red colour, with good body and a pleasantly bitter aftertaste. When young, the wine has a fruity taste, while it releases considerably refined perfumes when aged.

So the pleasingly fresh and slightly bitter aftertaste, as demonstrated in many tests carried out on different types of Brunello during the phase of refinement in wooden casks, is a varietal characteristic that the vine confers to the wine and which may accompany it for a long period of time in the bottle. It is therefore not a defect, but a quality that permits certain palates to identify the product and place it more correctly within the ambit of research for typical traits. In Italy Sangiovese is present in 67 provinces and 17 regions and occupies 10% of the entire vine-growing area, for a total of 7.3 million shoots. In Tuscany, Sangiovese is present in 38 denomination of origin wines (of which 5 are controlled and guaranteed denominations of origin and 6 are of protected geographical indication).

The strong push towards clone selection to support the need to renew vineyards with genetically tested material has been largely realised in this territory. The research for biotypes with good behavioural traits and resistance to stress, which are capable of producing a wine with good potential for aging, has seen the commitment of agronomists, enologists and breeders in the 'construction' of selected plants from the best Montalcino vineyards. The new clones of Sangiovese available for producers of Brunello therefore originate from vines that have produced the best in terms of product quality, and are synergically oriented towards increasingly precise productive trends and environmental propensities, even in relation to the real production per hectare obtainable in 'lose' terrain such as this,

79 - Montalcinese
ceramic pitcher and glass,
12th century, private collection

80 - pause during the harvest

81 - reshly harvested grapes

82 - Sant'Angelo in Colle, ➡
rainbow over the vineyards

which oscillates between 4000 and 6000 kilos per hectare; much less that the maximum ceiling foreseen by production regulations, which set the limit at 8000 kilos.

The range of clone choices available today is very wide and among the material suitable for replanting, the clones of Sangiovese with the Montalcino denomination, obtained with weak selection pressure, a technique that does not seek superlative performance of individual selections, but rather the performance of the different biotypes, represent a large segment of the products made available to breeders, which have been widely employed in this area in recent years.

All of the most famous enologists currently involved with wine-producers in this region have had to come to terms with this vine, which may express its best characteristics with some difficulty during the phase of vinification, given the great variety of vines.

This is why Giacomo Tachis 'the alchemist of Sassicaia', prefers it in combination with other varieties. According to the great enologist, the polyphenolic patrimony of Sangiovese is interesting, but not abundant, and this is in contrast with an 'international' enology. This evaluation is not confirmed by the opinion of other important colleagues, who stress the positive evolution when used pure, in relation to the territory, the growth of systems of cultivation and wine-producing techniques, and the improvement of the genetic material utilised today.

From this series of relationships, the most important local wine, obtained from Sangiovese grosso grapes and denominated Brunello, fully confirms the individual potential of this vine, due to its international profile and not only to its taste.

from vineyard to cellar

The mysterious alchemy that gives origin to wine requires long and careful work by wine-producers, in caring for the vineyard, choosing the most suitable grapes and processing in the wine cellar

5

83 - from the vineyard to the wine cellar, Altesino vineyard

84 - Lombard artists, 'Aurucnus', miniature in *Tacuinum Sanitatis*, parchment code, mid-14th century, Florence, National Library

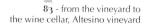

From vineyard to cellar

"The vine fell to its ruin with the aged tree, having grown old upon its bark, and, for the sad company it kept, was obliged to pass away with it".

Leonardo da Vinci, *'The vine and the old tree'* (Arundel, 42v)

85 - Leonardo da Vinci, *'Self-portrait'* (1512), Torino, Biblioteca reale

Acclimatised and cultivated with care for many years by local growers, vines have only recently become an emblem of wealth, and not only of material wealth, in the sunny, mineral rich hills of the Ilcinese chain. This took place gradually, passing from one vine to another, from one type to another, according to the changing canons of taste in various ages, but always guaranteeing a distinct territorial personality, notwithstanding the fact that the area gravitates in the vicinity of the boundless land of Chianti. In our own day Brunel-

lo holds this banner of typicality high. Adjusting to the rhythms of the era of telecommunications, the

wine has changed its image, becoming irresistible, unreachable and less ill tempered towards a market divided into limited segments. Da Vinci's short parable fits the mentality of this proud district well, as great care is taken to prevent the trees that support their gold-producing vines from growing too old. The vitacee family of plants, in fact, is expanding everywhere in the temperate zones of the planet.

Grafted and grown with care, each sub-species produces rich and sweet bunches, from which various wines are produced – white, rosé or red, sweet, dry or sparkling – all of which are valuable. Until a few years ago they were precious for their nutritional value and were a primary element in the diet of our ancestors.

Today they are precious for the pleasure they give us in tasting or combining them with traditional dishes or high international cuisine.

But wine is wine, even if it is called Brunello, so its history can be traced. And this traceability demands, through the heralds of the wine's original history, to be taken into consideration, in spite of the inevitable structural changes it has periodically undergone.

The first proposals to produce Brunello, a red wine obtained with extremely restrictive and innovative methods, from the agronomic and enological points of view, developed at the beginning of the 19th century, a period that saw the process of dissolution of the European viticultural patrimony, due to a radical American parasite, better known as phylloxera. Once the remedy was found – grafting cultivatable varieties on a base of American vine, a wild species not suitable for the production of grapes but for transformation – the patrimony of vineyards that had disappeared was rebuilt, along with the very

88 - work in the vineyard, depicted in a medieval print

89 - barbed cord cultivation system

concepts of viticulture, vinification and commerce, as the health of the vine was taken into consideration, rather than what the market wanted. The value and quality of the wine obtainable was considered, rather than the quantity that could be sold.

The intuition of one hundred years ago in the Montalcino country-side was destined to be a precursor of the times in the inevitable revolution of the entire national viticulture panorama. The old tree that wed the vine had fallen. It was time to give the vine a different type of support.

The genetic material, agronomical and wine cellar systems necessarily had to change their outlook and seek the road to profound renewal of methods and prospects. The regularly planted vineyards that

90 - new vineyard plantation in the area of San Sigismondo

91 - pruning shears

can be admired around Montalcino and which comb the landscape, chasing ideal geographical pathways, are the evolution of this manner of understanding the future. In this sense, the advantage of Brunello, which for a century had based its very

92 - gathering the grapes at the harvest time

93 - resting during the harvest

94 - harvest

existence on total quality, a concept that nobody today would ever dream of arguing about, appears unattainable by any other Italian wine.

FROM THE VINEYARD TO THE WINE CELLAR

A day almost never passes in the sun drenched Sangiovese grosso vineyards that make up the architectural framework of the Brunello di Montalcino hills, that the scores of workers do not carry out some important operation for the cultivation. In winter they are busy with pruning – the operation that will guarantee, freezing temperatures or hail permitting – the right number of bunches of grapes to send to vinification. But it is during the festive time of the harvest that the hillside slopes are coloured with the greatest number of industrious, vociferous workers.

The most widespread system of vine growing in this area is barbed wire. The trunk of the plant can reach a metre in height; then it stretches out horizontally to reach the vine growing alongside. The vine develops on three wires stretched between poles that support the plants. The first is the supporting wire and the other wires support the vegetation.

Another system is the Guyot. This method of pruning took its name from the researcher who described it for the first time almost one hundred years ago. The system uses a low trunk with a graft having

two gems, which then become two vine shoots, and a fruited cap that can have up to ten gems, which will support the great-est part of the pro-

duction. The vine develops on three wires, one of which is a bearing wire, supporting the fruited part, and the oth-er two, to which the shoots are tied.

In other rare cases a partic-ular posture may be imposed upon the vine, which is identi-fied with the term Alberello (n.t. small tree).

In this case the trunk of the vine is limited to a height varying between 30 and 50 cm, with 2, 3 or 4 branches with shoots of one or two buds each. Thus, the plant's development is con-trolled. Production is limited to a small number of bunches, which are, however, rich in sugars, and which determine the optimum alcohol content of the wine. This system rarely requires the use of poles.

At the moment of harvest, the pickers gather the grapes, selecting them according to the type of use foreseen and the degree of maturation desired for one or another particular type of vinification. The grapes are kept whole as much as possible. They are sent to the cellar, where the vines are removed and

the grapes are pressed. Today, machines are used that guarantee the necessary delicacy, and which do not provoke too much pressure. This would smash the skins excessively and break the vines, which could release unwanted green tannins to the must before being eliminated. In the vats, the marc obtained in this manner is mixed with the fermenting must, and maceration begins.

The increase in temperature takes place in an observable manner as early as the second day, and the must has to be frequently mixed again to maintain an optimal temperature between 25 and 28 °C. If the temperature is respected, after about a week of turbulent fermentation, the must has transformed almost all of the sugars into alcohol, which provokes extraction of the polyphenols, especially the tannins. A few days after fermentation is finished, the wine is drawn off, that is to say the must flower is separated from the marc, which will be pressed to extract residual wine that has remained in the skins. The wine obtained in this manner is very harsh and aggressive and will be softened a bit only upon completion of malolactic fermentation.

98 - corkscrews

99 - fermenting must

At this point the most important part of the evolution of Brunello in the wine cellar begins. During the years the wine must remain in casks the processes necessary to control its development are reduced to a minimum. Decanting is limited to three times during the first year and two times during successive years, and refilling ensures that the level of wine does not diminish, to avoid even minimal contact with the outside atmosphere. The variations in colour, from the typical ruby red of young wine to the garnet of aged wine, are progressively seen in the majority of the wine as the typical Brunello properties of taste and perfume emerge.

100 - thermally controlled stainless steel containers

101 - decanting in the cellar

Finally, the distinctive traits that guarantee the wine's success are confirmed in the dark, fresh environment of the cellar, through the long months of aging in the inert container of the bottle.

THE RULES OF PRODUCTION

Brunello is not an enological prodigy, but simply a product of the love for things well done that inspires the entire Ilcinese community, which can also be identified, first and foremost, but not only, in the care with which the regulations were written for the production of the denomination of Brunello di Montalcino wine of controlled and guaranteed origin (docg).

Among the reflections and aromas in a glass of Brunello, the light of the areas where its production is permitted shines through, the lands that must possess the precise traits that determine its identity:

never on the plains, never too rich in organic substances, always exposed to ensure proper development of the grapes, whose maximum quantity must be limited to 8,000 kilos per hectare, for a wine production of slightly more than 5,400 litres.

These numbers may seem high today, when growers are preoccupied with obtaining a suitable concentration to create the structure of a great modern red wine, something that is very much in vogue internationally, whether inspired or not by the capricious evolutions of the market.

The majority of Brunello producers don't get over 6,000 – 7,000 kilos per hectare, as they ignore general indications and lower the maximum quantity obtained through techniques such as green harvesting or pruning

102 - selection of grapes at the Col d'Orcia agricultural company

103 - pruning

to a smaller number of buds, even though docg wine came of age some time ago, having been recognised in 1980 and improved in 1998.

The structure obtained in this manner, that is to say the compendium of the wine's various components, is always very full bodied, thanks to the pedo-climatic conditions, which are extremely variable in Montalcino.

The limit of 8,000 kilos per hectare in fact appears valid, since the new planting methods, already extensively applied in this area, foresee a greater density of stalks per hectare.

While all of this respects optimal physiological conditions and permits much lower individual production of grapes, even only a kilo per plant, it also

104 - vineyard and farmhouse in Tavernelle

105 - Col d'Orcia company vineyard

106 - pieces of wood used to keep metallic wires supporting vines taut

generally helps vineyards reach the maximum limits set by the regulation, joining as it does the concepts of quantity, albeit limited, and quality.

THE SLOPES

Those who consider Bacchus' nectar only a red or white industrial drink would wrinkle their nose at the different traits Brunello di Montalcino presents from one vineyard to another – which they would consider traits to be evaluated in the most improbable guides, by arbitrary parameters – especially since this is a homogeneous product, thanks to the vinification of only Sangiovese grapes, the limited territory where it is grown and the application of severe rules of production.

But the difference is inevitable when you produce the same wine in environments that have such diverse microclimatic characteristics as those that make up the 'Sangiovese pyramid', as the Montalcino hills have been defined. The area of production can be divided into four principle zones, the slopes where differences are not so strongly noticeable.

To the north, the seasons are more clear-cut, of the continental type, and the northerly winds lower the winter temperature by several degrees. The terrain is discreetly fertile, richer than elsewhere, and is fresh and loose. The Brunellos produced in this area are more perfumed and robust in body.

107 - vine leaves wet with dew

To the west, the westerly marine breezes release their salty temperament to the grapes. The terrain is rougher here, more broken up, ventilated and stony, but there is also clay. With all of this mineral variety, the wine is always quite savoury.

The terrain looking south is located in an ideally shaped glen, protected from the dominating winds. The average temperature is higher, which produces advancement in the vegetative activity of the vines. In this area precipitation is more rare and the terrain is more permeable, rich with calcareous skeletal material, not very fertile, dry and hard to cultivate. Here the rustic characteristics of the vine are fully exalted. The strength of the alcohol content distinguishes Brunello wine produced on these slopes. The highest altitudes in the area are reached to the east, on the terraces facing Mount Amiata. Winds batter the area and contribute to keeping the air healthful. The terrain is varied, with ample cretaceous areas mixed with sand and ravine formations. The wine is genuine and expresses its roundest traits.

AGING

The five-year aging process of Brunello hypothesized by the Clemente Santi family quite some time before our own day, which is described in the regulations currently applied, is founded on the obligation for the wine to age in barrels or durmast casks (which, following the corrections made in 1998, are no longer of obligatory size) for at least two years (three years for reserve).

108 - wood used to build casks

The wine must then age for at least another four months in the bottle, rigorously of the Bordeaux type (six months for reserve) before it can be labelled and claim its rightful place on the market.

The progressive abandonment of large barrels, which have increasingly been substituted by small casks of the French barrique type, is a phenomenon that is also taking place in Montalcino and that inspires discussion among producers because of the great personality of Brunello, obtained through the respect of original formulas, which includes a predilection for traditional vats of large dimensions.

These barrels have a discreet and complex relationship with the wine. The release of vanilla taste is more imperceptible and the robustness of the wine is exalted, but care must be taken to avoid problems and unwanted tastes. Additionally, the size of the mass conservable in the large barrels does not allow very fast exchange between the wine and the external atmosphere, thereby slowing the process of oxidation that makes the product age too quickly. The difference is evident and some ask whether the barrique is not disrupting the very character of this wine, given its ability to refine it more rapidly. The questions everyone is asking today are: will Brunello in barriques be ready to drink sooner and will it then possess the notes of knowing boisé – will it perhaps be easier on the consumer's palate, will it stand up under prolonged aging?

Most Montalcino producers are halfway between the decision to abandon the large vats and repudiate the small cask. In the Ilcinese wine cellars the suggestive barrels, in some cases really enormous and still used today, are surrounded by 228 litre

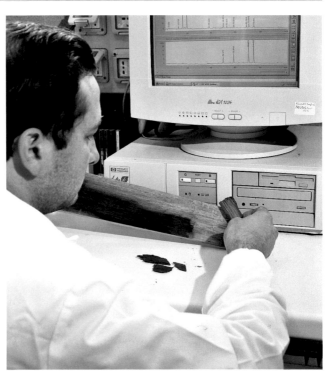

109 - analysing wood

French wood, and the Brunello is transferred from one to the other according to the opinion of the enologists in charge.

Few wines in the world can boast of an ability to stand up under aging similar Brunello di Montalcino's, and the periodical, interesting tasting sessions of old and very old vintages have confirmed this renowned characteristic.

As time goes by the colour of Brunello changes, from intense ruby red to garnet, to the point that it sometimes acquires shades of orange. A net change towards brick red indicates that the wine is 'maderized' – that is to say that oxidation has provoked the end of a bottle's potential for aging. So to avoid losing value, old bottles are checked through a practice known as refilling. Bottles that

110 - Argiano Estate cellar

111 - tasting Brunello

112 - 60 and 120-hectolitre casks

113 - barrique

show a slight decrease in the level of the liquid are uncorked. The quality of the contents is checked and the volume of the wine is restored to the correct level by filling it back up from another previously uncorked bottle.

The decanting of the small amounts necessary to refill the bottles is performed through simple, ancient methods such as 'pumping' a term used in rural Tuscany to define the utilisation of a thin, perforated straw with one extremity free and the other inserted in the pocket of air that is created inside the neck of the bottle when it is tipped, to avoid turbulence that would move the eventual deposit at the bottom of the bottle. At the end of this extremely delicate operation the bottle is re-corked, using a new cork, since older wine is more fragile.

It goes without saying that corks must pass quality tests of every possible and imaginable kind, since we are dealing with bottles that are worth several thousand euro, like in the case Franco Biondi Santi's del Greppo vineyard.

The bouquet and taste of Brunello are continuously modified during aging. The fruited aroma of the young wine becomes increasingly faint; the bouquet, that is the set of olfactory sensations that a mature wine produces, becomes more intense, acquiring delicacy and consequently greater value.

When you approach a very old bottle of wine, you must be aware that time has left testimony that must not be read with today's canons. The wine is a relic of a 'distant' past in terms of technology, however short it may be in terms of years. It is the grape juice of that time, fermented and refined in the great wooden casks of the time, vinified with the means of that time, when air circulated freely. Remixing was performed with manual pumps and the contribution of chemical analysis was reduced to a minimum. But the harmonious perfume and softness to the palate do not change.

114 - old winepress

One of the challenges of Brunello is still to be recalled, together with the breath of the land and its people, even after the passage of many years.

THE RESERVE

The production of Brunello Reserve is obtained from the best grapes, selected during harvest under the vigil eyes of the producer. The must has to have the right sugar content and processing must permit the wine to reach an alcoholic content 0.5 greater than the basic product.

With an additional year of aging before being marketed and an enhanced structure that steps up the organoleptic properties of this choice wine, reminiscent of the rich bunches selected from all of the authorised vineyards, this is the most sought-

115 - old wooden bunghole

116 - old winepress ➡

after result. Reserve cannot be produced every year. The grapes must be whole to attain this category and this doesn't happen in unfavourable years, when atmospheric agents or other adverse factors hinder complete ripening and a robust structure of the wine.

In fact, the peculiar exposition of vineyards that enjoy optimal microclimatic situations, even in common years, permits some vineyards to produce Reserve, even though it might not be considered possible elsewhere, perhaps just a few kilometres away.

Often, despite the bad name a particularly hard year might generally confer on wines, some producers may decide to select a small share of their

grapes for prolonged aging, for an additional year, and thus list the Brunello obtained in the highest category.

THE OLD VINTAGES

The bottles chosen for tasting are placed upright almost eight days prior to uncorking, to allow decanting of all the deposits formed through the years. The ideal temperature for tasting has to be reached slowly and progressively, preparing the bottle for uncorking and taking care to cover the neck with the capsule so that it is closed, but not hermetically, in the room where the tasting is to take place.

The temperature in this environment must not be above 18° C, at least 24 hours before the tasting, to allow eventual chemical-olfactive structures to leave room for the actual opening of the wine. De-

117 - 'Host uncorking a bottle', nineteenth century painting by Federigo Andreotti

118 - drawing off a sample

canting is performed before the tasting. It is advisable for the decanting to be performed accurately and allow a brief wait of a few minutes, as the evolution of the perfumes begins as soon as the bottle is uncorked and it is not a good idea to miss further passages. Usually, the taster should spend a good hour on a wine that has aged for a long period of time. Commentary must take into account the characteristics of the dating and the events that marked the year in question (climate, progress of vegetation, company situation, harvests, vinifications, etc.).

On considering the aspect of the wine, the taster will note the less lively and more faded colours and lights with respect to younger wines. Ruby red will give way to tones tending to orange and, even if the aspect does not appear encouraging, judgement must be objective, because these wines reserve their best surprises for the sense of smell. The aromas that develop are more tenuous and ethereal than those of a young wine, and more difficult to identify. The bouquet, developed through phenomena of oxide reduction during the period of aging in the bottle, allows the aromas to appear complex and evasively receding.

Although several glorious old vintages generally offer rich, powerful aromas, the so-called intermediate vintages are characterised more by subtlety than by the richness and complexity of the bouquet.

Several aged wines seem perhaps less alcoholic and slightly more acid to the palate, because harvests were once moved to the earliest possible date, given the lack of sufficient hygienic protection; often, a high level of volatile acidity may be detected, which is more intense than what may be noticeable in new wines in our own day.

The reasons for this are the less perfect and severe conditions under which the wine was cultivated and vinified, with respect to the present: malolactic fermentation drawn out over a long period of time,

120 - vine leaves

121 - old Biondi Santi Brunello vintages

extremely old barrels, lack of control of vinification temperature, re-mixing methods that favoured oxidation, insufficiently insulated cellars, and so forth.

Fifteen to twenty year old wines still have fine qualities of structure, are neither lean nor dry, but long ago lost the basic fruitiness of their youth, of which there is only a hint in the fading sweet tones of the bouquet. Oak or vanilla aromas may still be detected, but are muted by the overlying perfume of underbrush, truffles, jam, coffee, smoke and pine pitch.

Wines over 20 years old may develop olfactive components, as a function of the dating, which inspire enthusiasm. Both to the sense of smell and taste, one may detect notes of rose or peony, but coffee, citrus fruit or mint may also be evoked.

122 - 'The two youngsters saved by St. Niccolò', fifteenth century Sienese sculptor. The legend relates how they fell into the sea while playing on the beach. They were saved by St. Niccolò, however, who sent them a demijohn, which was once used alternatively to contain pickled olives and wine

NEW AND OLD CELLARS

When many company's increase in size, wine cellars must also inevitably adjust.

Small, medium sized and large companies have given rise to this development, with the result that more than 65% of Monalcino's wine cellars have presented plans or completed remodelling projects, which have even been monumental in some cases, with an average territorial investment of more than 150 thousand euro.

A wine cellar of the historical type that digs into the ground and branches out in various meandering corridors is no longer functional for modern vinification and conservation of wines; such a place, however, is still capable of expressing the suggestive

123 - a modern laboratory for analyses

charm that derives from the care taken in building the place and the ingenious architectural solutions invented by master artisans to guarantee that those bygone enological practices were carried out in an adequate facility.

These cellars still have the perfume of the live stone upon which they are founded, of the robust and powerful wines that were stored there, of the essence of various woods which, stacked in an orderly manner, conserved the grapes and must.

Today's new wines, on the other hand, are stored in larger facilities of modern conception, capable of housing advanced technologies and offering maximum guarantees of cleanliness, hygiene, conservability and practicality.

Modern Montalcino wine producing cellars are often almost hidden and detached from the rest of the company facilities. They are dug underground, not far from the ancient walls that host the dwellings of the winegrowers, and are made of strong and appropriately insulated prefabricated building units, manufactured from steels, agglomerates and extremely solid tiles, and have high ceilings and air acclimatisation. In these modern caverns, Brunello wine is born, developed and lovingly nurtured, with the care necessary for its lengthy and correct development, once it has abandoned its native terrain.

Behind the old historical cellars' solid wood doors, there is the risk of abandonment; the rhythms of modern life are too frenetic. There are too many other company priorities to take care of before they can plan a dignified retirement for the aging underground rooms, where there are still vats, flasks and bottles of wine from the thin vines once cultivated promiscuously.

But there are solutions. Historical companies are aware of the cul-

124 - control station for bottling operations

125 - information technology systems in a modern analyses laboratory

126 - modern equipment from the Argiano Estate

tural and artistic importance of this building patrimony, even though it is not entirely obsolete for the storage of wine, and tend to preserve such buildings from abandonment and oblivion, even creating wine museums to accentuate the intense atmosphere and realising artistic and cultural events for visitors, among whom they may evidently also promote Brunello di Montalcino commercially.

THE FUTURE OF FUTURES

127 - bottling

The progressive evolution of the product, due to the reduced time it remains in the barrels and the diversification of types of woods utilised, has not failed to inspire discussion, even in the national and international press.

Internationally, the position is generally opposite that of the Italians. Perhaps they are worried abroad to see the universal values of Brunello being lost, which for many commentators would be something to count as part of humanity's patrimony, like urban centres with monumental complexes,

historical buildings and landscapes that are recognised as being unique in the world.

Harvest year 1995, the first year that allowed producers to reduce the period of aging in wooden casks, has evidently become a fundamental date to understand what is happening in Montalcino, where the contradiction between acceleration and refinement and several counter positions at the vanguard of economical manouevres in connection with the product have given rise to perplexities, even among authoritative personalities tied to the history of the local enological jewel, such as Biondi Santi, Stefano Cinelli Colombini and Piero Talenti.

The formula of purchasing Brunello en primeur, which several Ilcinese companies began in the nineties, that is to say the sale of bottles several years before they are marketed, is quite an uncertain procedure. This formula permits the purchaser to acquire lots at an advantageous price, despite paying in advance and to guarantee the availability of wine that is difficult to find.

The practice, nevertheless, is reserved to a limited number of producers, who are capable of guaranteeing qualitative levels of excellence, to

PRIMEUR
ALTESINO
AVIGNONESI

CERTIFICATO DI PRENOTAZIONE
N.   RILASCIATO A:

Relativo all'acquisto dei seguenti vini:
BRUNELLO DI MONTALCINO 1985
VINO NOBILE DI MONTEPULCIANO 1985
che saranno consegnate dopo l'invecchiamento

DATA

128 - a specimen of Primeur

constantly reach greater international recognition, with the consequent economic valorisation of the product over the years.

Economic paper, called futures, represent lots of six bottles and, although they are in the name of a specific person, they are in fact negotiable by the bearer and therefore may be sold to others. They are issued by several wine producers and by the Consortium of producers, and give holders the right to exchange them for the wine at a certain date of expiration. The contract takes concrete form upon marketing of the wine, after the five years foreseen by the reference norms. In supporting this operation, the purchaser wagers on the wine and the seriousness of the firm, making an investment on the basis of the potential qualitative growth of the product and trademark over the years.

The economic evaluation of the future of Brunello, translated into stock market language, appears to be ill adapted with the murmurings of lowering levels of the product's savouriness, due to the push to make it drinkable in the shortest time possible.

In wine growing companies in the area, there are enologists and agronomists of great prestige, such as Franco Bernabei, Maurizio Castelli, Stefano Chioccioli, Roberto Cipresso, Nicolò d'Afflitto, Carlo Ferrini, Vittorio Fiore, Giulio Gambelli, Pablo Harri, Attilio Pagli, Pietro Rivella, Giacomo Tachis, Paolo Vagaggini and many more, who represent the best that Tuscany and Italy can offer in this field.

The presence of these people, with their baggage of professional knowledge and experience, has until now ensured the fine quality of Brunello and Montalcino wines in general, and they are also a guarantee of quality in future.

WHERE IS BRUNELLO GOING?

Brunello of Montalcino, which the prestigious American magazine Wine Spectator has listed among the twelve best wines of the twentieth century, is what passionate wine lovers buy most in our country, regardless of the fact that the price of a bottle is among the highest, with respect to the vast majority of wines present on the market.

The question of the price per bottle of quality wine produced in certain regions and of Brunello di Montalcino in particular, has always interested lovers of good drinking. What determines the price of a bottle of Brunello di Montalcino?

To better evaluate the question the increase in company costs must be taken into consideration. They must periodically equip themselves with suitable wine making instruments, and they have capital immobilised in maturing wine. A variable must

129 - vineyard near Montalcino

be added to this that is difficult to determine. What is the added value of a series of formal and substantial commercial supports: a proposal of style in the trademark, visibility of the company personality, aesthetic factors, evolved communications and cultural contributions? These are elements that have a variable, but definitely considerable cost.

Facing the overall costs of superior quality wine means marking up consumer prices; given the research to create an image in this territory, it is also based on the synergy among all the economic components involved. The range of prices throughout the denomination naturally occupies the entire segment of medium-high prices. But the willingness to buy shown by a large segment of consumers confirms that Brunello is in any case a good deal.

Nevertheless the range is wide. Even though we start from a high market segment, there is a difference of 400% between the cheapest and most expensive bottles. This shows the greater commitment of firms oriented in the highest segment to face considerable additional costs, without saving on commercial policies, on the reduction of the quantity available, the assertion of the trademark, on promotional instruments and, finally on the sales organisation itself.

The greater cost of Brunello with respect to other wines is not al-

130 - Montalcino, Civic and Diocese Museum of Sacred Art, *'Madonna with Child crowned by two angels, St. John the Baptist and Peter'*, Andrea Della Robbia (Florence, 1435-1525), glass-veined earthenware. In the left column there is a bunch of grapes

ways indicative of quality. Wine that costs more is not necessarily better; it will definitely have been produced with global criteria of quality, with great care in its formal aspects. It will have a large and well-articulated company structure behind it, rich in human resources, or it will be the fruit of the passion of a single wine grower who owns a small vineyard, cultivated as if it were a jewel.

On the contrary, a cheaper Brunello may be the result of company management and size, which could compress production costs, or be the result of an attempt to position a company on the market.

The new production regulations, which took effect in 1998, allow enlargement of the area of cultivation, authorising vineyards of 2.000 hectares, against the 1.250 of past years. Thanks to the long aging and simultaneous growth of vine shoots, the new Brunello di Montalcino plants require a good number of years to become economically viable, but the doubling of the quantity of docg wine foreseen for the next decade worries wine growers. Most of the new companies in Montalcino belong to larger companies, but the most important ones in Italy, from Antinori to Folonari, from Frescobaldi to Gaja, which have powerful foreign participation like the United States winegrowers Marini and Mondavi, have already been increasing their local productive capacity for some time now.

131 - glass of Brunello

The other wines
of montalcino

Brunello di Montalcino is not
the only wine produced in the area.
In this chapter we shall also speak
of Rosso, Moscadello, sant'Antimo
and vin santo

6

132 - 'new' wine coming from the press

133 - red and white grapes

134 - bottle of Banfi Moscadello

The other wines of Montalcino

MOSCADELLO DI MONTALCINO

After the powerful success of the Sangiovese vine had given Montalcino a shining emblem with deep red tones, the reawakening of Moscadello, a wine produced with Moscato grapes, was a foregone conclusion. The enological history of these territories, in fact, describes a situation that was also oriented towards other chromatic reflections, such as the golden tones of Moscadello. Moscadello was the most famous local wine for many centuries, with which the inhabitants of the villages and the rural families quenched their thirst, and to which important therapeutic virtues were attributed, including what was considered an almost thaumaturgical quality during those times, of contributing to the healing of persons stricken with the plague. The production of Moscadello has ancient origins. In 1540, in a letter sent to a friend, writer Pietro Aretino thanked him for the gift of a *"keg of precious, delicate Moscadello, round and light"*, while several documents in the secret Vatican Archives in Rome testify to the fact that in the land holdings that were the property of the Abbacy of Sant'Antimo, in 1591, a certain quantity of Moscadello was already being produced, and several decades later, Pope Urbano VIII expressed a high opinion of the wine *"for its vigorousness and flavour"* and, with great discretion, *"he often requested it for himself and for his court"*.

High praise for this wine is never missing from travel books and accounts of wayfarers between the seventeenth and nineteenth centuries, as it was considered *"among the rarest and most renowned wines of Tuscany"*. In 1685, Francesco Redi sung its praises in the pages of his famous booklet entitled *Bacchus in Tuscany*, written in honour of the best Tuscan wines:

"Of the lovely little,
of the oh, so divine, little
'Moscadelletto'
of Montalcino. "

Redi himself, given the international fame he had reached at the time, defined it *"wine that is full of grace, for the ladies of Paris and for those so beautiful as to cheer up the Thames"*.

Bartolomeo Gherardini, auditor for the Grand Duke of Tuscany Cosimo III, wrote in 1676: *"The ex-*

135 - the historical recognition assigned Biondi Santi for Moscadello at the Exposition Universelle of Paris in 1867

136 - 'Taster', Philip Merciet, 1730

portation of the above-mentioned Moscadello, which is very famous for its delicacy and subtlety, brings money to the city, even taking into account the expenses of cultivation; it is the auditor's opinion that the expense equals the earnings". This simple evaluation clearly indicates the difficulty of producing this wine – difficulties which are still partially extant today, both in the cellar and the vineyard.

In his Florentine sojourn, Ugo Foscolo advised friends and relatives to drink Moscadello.

Between the nineteenth and twentieth centuries, the diseases most loathed by winegrowers throughout the world, oidium, peronospora and, above all, phylloxera, brought about a sudden end to the centuries-old cycle of old Moscadello vines, as it infected nearly the entirety of those perfectly rectangular parcels, planted in deep, well drained trenches, surrounded by hedges that defended them from wild animals and herds.

The grapes of these 'parcels of civilisation', as they were called by Cosimo de' Medici III, were prevalently given over to two types of vinification: the 'champagne' method, as it was called until the end of the nineteenth century, and the method of ex-siccation. Soft pressing had been advised for many centuries in both methods. Filtering followed, and the wine was allowed to rest until the first cold weather, when it was bottled in flasks.

Nevertheless, Moscadello did not entirely disappear, even though its production gradually diminished. At the beginning of the '90s, there were only 10,000 surviving stalks of Moscadello in Montalcino, casually arranged on 7 hectares of land.

Today, due to the type of 'late harvest' the most interesting from the organoleptic point of view, the production of partially dried grapes must not

137 - Moscadello bunches

138, 139 and 140 - Fifteenth century straw-lined flask, contemporary reproduction; Tuscan flask with straw lining, 18th century; straw-lined Tuscan flask, 18th century, museum of glass

141 - vine trunk

exceed 5,000 kg per hectare and the harvest may not start before the first of October of each year. The minimum alcohol content permitted for consumption is 15°. About 100,000 bottles are produced annually, from 80 hectares of land planted with this vine, but this is not to be confused with the more than 150 doc wines that are produced with Moscato grapes in the Mediterranean basin and in Eastern Europe, thanks to its extremely recognisable aroma, which is more stable with one of the three types of harvests foreseen by regulations, namely the late harvest.

In addition to the emergence of the phenomenon of 'wines for meditation', which laid the basis for international interest in sweet, liquor-like wines, the recognisable and typical traits of this aroma demand serious reflection on the possibilities for commercial success of Moscadello. Such international interest brought about the rethinking of the structure of the wine, and many of the vineyards earmarked for the production of sparkling Moscadello are being converted to offer selected grapes for late harvest.

The result is a golden, aromatic and sweet, but not too sweet wine, alongside one of the most important red wines in the international enological panorama.

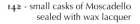

142 - small casks of Moscadello sealed with wax lacquer

143 - Castelnuovo dell'Abate, ➡ high relief, detail of the Sant'Antimo Abbacy façade

SANT'ANTIMO

It seems incredible that in such a prestigious territory, thanks to three important vines that are recognised everywhere, Brunello, Rosso and Moscadello, vast cultivations of vines that are not governed by regulations produce a generic wine. There is also unexploited winegrowing potential on the western slopes of the half-moon hillside that surrounds Montalcino from the Orcia Valley to the Vigne Plains, up to Buonconvento. The terrain is mixed, alluvial, but also rich in skeletal elements. It is good land for vines of various origins, which are at least as famous as the Sangiovese. The penetration of 'improved' vines, as they were called before the term 'international' was coined, such as Cabernet or Chardonnay, and the diffusion of Merlot, already present in vast areas of the Italian peninsula, was a phenomenon that was followed with attention by the local winegrowing community, to avoid being excluded from enological trends in fashion, and sometimes only to avoid giving the impression of being overly conservative.

On 18 January 1996, the fourth reserved denomination in the territory of Montalcino was officially recognised with a Ministry of Agriculture decree that used an extremely innovative formula for the Italian system of the day, which was explained by the proven quality of wines produced outside the dominant denominations and the need to further improve quality.

Sant'Antimo was added to Rosso, Moscadello and Brunello docg, supplying a coverage of excellence for the entire winegrowing area within the municipal territory of Montalcino. The creation of the wine involved the long commitment of one of the most brilliant 'thinkers of wine' of recent years, the enologist Ezio Rivella, who, in addition to the alchemy exercised over his wines, amalgamating enological and commercial theories, hypothesized and sustained, in common agreement with the in-

144 - vine leaves clinging
to the vine

145 - Castelnuovo dell'Abate,
view of the Sant'Antimo Abbacy

terested producers and with the protective consortiums, an original le-vel of total quality, which brought about the birth of Sant'Antimo doc.

This permitted the firms to experiment new wines, both red and white, based on mixed grapes of the international style, among which there was the insertion of Sangiovese, well positioned and favoured in the percentages, thanks also to the possibility that the producers had of earmarking the same grapes of Brunello or Rosso di Montalcino in the composition of new wines.

In addition to the vastness of the territory involved, even the ampelographic base of reference

146 - decanter and glasses ➡
for tasting of Brunello

is very large and includes all of the vines recommended or authorised in the Province of Siena. This has determined the creation of wines with extremely different characteristics from each other, with a wide array of tastes and range. And there is the possibility of anticipating the market with 'new' wine ('novello').

The choice for consumers is also facilitated by the specifications permitted on the label, which, alongside the original denominations, may also indicate the prevalent vine, among the types of Chardonnay, Pinot Grigio and Sauvignon for the white wines, and Cabernet, Merlot and Pinot Nero for the reds. Research in aging continues, the duration of which is not set by any standard, but follows the natural physiological maturation of the must. In the case of 'novello' wine, aging is cut short. Aging may be carried out in wooden containers having a maximum capacity of 5 hectolitres. The size, inspired by the traditional kegs used for Vin Santo, is also extended to the structured reds of Sant'Antimo. The wood chosen for the construction of the containers to associate with these wines may be chestnut, or perhaps cedar, Slavonian durmast oak,

147 - small vine leaves

spear wood or cherry, according to the aromatic choice preferred by the producer. The quercus genre is in any case prevalent, and the styles of production are exquisitely French. So Sant'Antimo doc not only makes the use of the barrique and the size greater than a ton official, in an environment that had until now considered them with great scepticism, but also grants these instruments an exclusive role in the production of several types of wine.

The regulations also provide for yield and alcohol content based on values similar to those for Brunello and Rosso, yields that guarantee a maximum mass of 63 hectolitres per hectare.

The regulations for the production of Sant'Antimo include wines without the specification of the vine and with the specification of the vine (Chardonnay, Sauvignon and Pinot Grigio for the whites and Cabernet Sauvignon, Merlot and Pinot Nero for the reds), in addition to Vin Santo and Vin Santo Occhio di Pernice. Several industrial wines are also included in this doc area – the latest of which are the already famous 'super Tuscan' wines – which the vineyards of Montalcino produce alongside Brunello and other traditional wines.

148 - Castelnuovo dell'Abate, Sant'Antimo Abbacy, capital of external column

149 - wine against the light

150 - Montalcino, the fortress

ROSSO DI MONTALCINO

The birth of Rosso di Montalcino as a doc wine goes back to 1984, but the first true leap in quality was accomplished in the nineties.

Most of the raw material comes from the same vineyards enrolled in the superior category, although many new plantations have been especially created to exalt the characteristics of this wine. During the phase of vinification, this wine has the prerogative of simply becoming a less structured red wine, less aged, ready to drink and capable of expressing all of the fruited and suave sensations that only a young, but authoritative wine can offer. From the commercial point of view, the definition Rosso di Montalcino has enabled local winegrowers to avoid freezing their capital for the long periods of time necessary for stocking and aging wine, by permitting more rapid exchange time.

The regulations also contain an innovation: for the first time in Italy, producers are allowed to obtain two doc wines from the same vineyards. In fact, the vineyards that produce Brunello may also be utilised for Rosso di Montalcino, while the limit for maximum yield remains 8,000 kilos per hectare and the reverse situation is not possible.

In the hectares earmarked only for Rosso, limited because of the lower level of quality obtainable, the maximum yield per hectare is 9,000 kilos, and the yield for transformation of grapes into wine must not be greater than 70%. Finally, as early as the advanced stage of vinification, if the wine does not appear to be evolving in the desired manner, it may be diverted to Rosso, labelled as such, but offering for con-sumption a less defined and less structured wine than the future Brunello would have been, with all of the qualities that derive from a careful selection of the wine, even in the cellar. Already appraised and known by several denominations, Rosso di Montalcino acquired a precise identity and official recognition with the passage to doc wine, which took place with a Decree of the President of the Republic on 25 November, 1983. Additionally, the new regulations, published in Official Gazette n° 148 of 26 June 1996, introduced, among the other innovations, the obligation to bot-

151 - harvest

tle the wine in the area and defined the term 'vine', in a manner analogous to French cru, that is to say with greater identification on the label of the product, obtained in a limited area, of which the superior quality is recognised, thanks to the favourable micro-climactic conditions, the age of the vineyards planted there and the enological results. Winemakers who wish to enrol a vineyard in this roll with a specific name, must guarantee that the grapes and wine derived respect the more restrictive norms with respect to the types without indications.

Rosso di Montalcino has grapes, agronomic and enological methods that are similar to Brunello,

152 - Bordeaux bottles

but which differentiate above all in the aging of the wine, which is limited to just one year, and in the minimum alcohol content, which is 12°. The primary fruited aromas are consequently different, being what the vine can express under the conditions of different and more oriented processing. Anyone who considers Rosso di Montalcino nothing more than an 'almost Brunello' does not fully understand its true essence, which makes it a substantially different wine.

Of course, the analogies between the two wines are numerous: the same territory, the same climate, the same grapes, the same winegrowers, the same basic methods, but the results are different.

153 - red autumn leaves

From the genuine tones of a young and vivacious wine, the palate and nostrils receive an extremely soft, velvety array of perfumes and tastes of sweet, mature grapes or solid, supportive and authoritative structure. This is precisely the element where the difference is most marked between Rosso and Brunello, which is capable of considerable differentiation within its category, although it always conserves a shared base that makes it easily identifiable, unless the trend toward an international taste prevails. It is easy to think that this homogeneous structure may be the result of prolonged aging in wood, which the doc variety does not have.

It is with legitimate perplexity that we wonder

whether Rosso, in coming years, may absorb the production of Brunello, and why the realisation of an innovative product, that expresses all of the characteristics of the Sangiovese vine in this territory, vinified in purity, is not included in the canons and forms of the Rosso, which permits more freedom of interpretation and possesses a quality-price ratio that exalts the first rate materials and local grapes. In fact, Rosso di Montalcino may be marketed the first of September in the year following production of the grapes, but this indication does not hinder its further aging, for several additional months.

The regulation also leaves ample freedom to producers, who may decide whether to age it in casks or not. It is therefore possible to find young Rosso on the market, fresh and frothy in its evolution in contact with the cold steel vats, or structured and complex Rosso, which reveals intimate contact with the oak cask, small or large as it may be.

The regulations for production also provide that wine suitable to become Brunello may be marketed during the period of aging as Rosso di Montalcino, if it is not deemed suitable for further aging in harmony with its category.

VIN SANTO

The people of Montalcino are not very fond of Vin Santo. There is Moscadello, the boasted pride of the area, with its sweetness and drinkability, which does not require the five tormented years necessary to produce one of the most ancient emblems of Tuscan enology. Nevertheless, Vin Santo is 'liquid tradition', and therefore the question is considered to be of a qualifying nature, at least by the vineyards that have a certain history. But this wine, with its extremely particular procedure of production, has recently been further ennobled in the area. Sant'Antimo doc has recreated the conditions for a titled and marketable production of the wine, according to the formal canons required.

The title of 'king of exsiccated wines' now attributed to Vin Santo derives from its organoleptic complexity. Present throughout the region, which conserves a great deal of diversity from one area to another, Vin Santo is the same everywhere and is always very recognisable. The distinctive note is the oxidized character obtained during the phase of aging, which is extremely pleasant,

154 - 14th century miniature depicting three persons drinking wine from bottles, flasks and glasses, while the cellar man pours the wine and serves it

155 - small casks for the aging of Vin Santo

156 - the curious star-shaped disks used to stretch the metallic wires that support the vines

but which can also be a source of dissatisfaction if has not been well controlled. This wine, which is also obtained from red grapes – in this case it takes the name of 'occhio di pernice' – remains tied to the image of white grapes, placed to exsiccate on grates or suspended in great earthen halls with wooden beams and crossbeams.

The base of Vin Santo has always been Trebbiano, but additions of Tuscan Malvasia or other white vines may exalt its aromatic characteristics. Once this concentration of sugary pulp is pressed, the must obtained is transferred to small, characteristic nosecone-shaped kegs; these small barrels, normally made of chestnut and often used for an excessive length of time, have recently begun to be replaced by the more practical barriques. The deposits from the previous vinification, which are called 'matrixes', are culled from the barriques and controlled for cleanliness, after which they are put into the new must. When the barrique is full, it is sealed with wax lacquer.

The formula applied for generations requires that the so-called 'vinsantaie' be stored in the attic. The storage places, detached from the body of the underlying dwelling, or created especially for the purpose, are exposed to the whims of climactic variations, differences in exposure, winds and freezing.

Several enological technicians suggest moving the kegs to the protected area of the cellar, where there would not be the great excursion in temperatures, of such a degree as to excessively influence the biological processes taking place in the evolution of the product; but many producers, faithful to traditional procedures, consider these proposals to be somewhat 'heretic'.

157 - 'cantucci' biscuits and Vin Santo, an ideal combination

Always according to tradition, the 'matrixes', that is to say the mucilaginous aggregated mass that forms from the amalgamated natural deposits during aging, upon which the wine rests, must be utilised for the next vinification; nevertheless, there are enologists who consider this practice with aversion, doubting its organoleptic validity. It was once a great concern to ensure that the wood did not have an overriding power over the wine and the use of small kegs was preferred, which were already exhausted by previous vinifications. Tasters suggest that we use new wooden containers, that is according to the latest and important world enology wine producing indicators, but the purists have asserted that the new wood aromas have had a negative effect on Vin Santo wine quality. It seems that this fine Tuscan wine owes its name to the saintly patience needed in production. But in the final analysis we often wonder at the quality of the wine.

158 - characteristic seal in wax for the Vin Santo casks

The land of Brunello

Following the perfume of Brunello
will lead you to discover the natural
beauty and the signs of art and
history, the patrimony of these
lands of great charm

7

MONTALCINO
ALT mt. 56h

159 - Montalcino, panorama

160 - Montalcino, sign entering town

The land of Brunello

161 and 162 - Etruscan artifacts: *oinochòes* (amphora for wine), mixing amphora and copper strainer, private collection

Montalcino has always shown that it has strong ties with the handful of villages that make up its suburbs, ties which are still maintained today through the production of Brunello and other types of extremely characteristic wines in the respective territories of these villages, all of which, however, can be traced to common roots, as expressed in the city's coat of arms. In past ages the various villages connected to Montalcino shared in the organisation of defence in the event of military attacks from 'abroad', since each of them was capable of supplying men, refuge and foodstuffs to withstand eventual siege, as well as artisan competence.

The various castles in the surrounding defensive line assumed the role of primary first line defence, according to the direction from which the danger might come in the surrounding territory.

At the end of sinuous roads, many of which are still unpaved today, the burgs and castles that made up the external ring of the city of Mon-

THE TERRITORY OF MONTALCINO

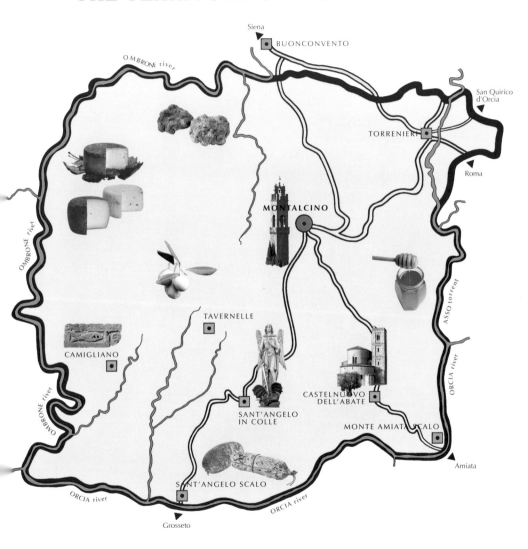

talcino are well-known, not only because of the wine produced in their respective territories, but also because they each have a history to recount, through their parishes, their noble palaces and families. Alongside the illustrious names of the inhabitants of these villages, history also takes us back to the profile of less conventional personalities, confusing these areas, together with the nearby maremma, with the cradle of Tuscan banditry in the nineteenth century.

Along the road that forks into two branches in the vicinity of Montalcino, the farms whose names

163 - Sienese crete

are often spoken by wine connoisseurs through-out the world pop up over the vineyard-laden hills and dales.

MONTALCINO

Who can fail to admire the beautiful homes that appear, perched on the hillsides, as they travel along the road, with its numerous hairpin turns that climb up towards Montalcino.

The sensation of finding oneself in a special place is very strong, and as you gradually ap-proach the city, enter the tiny historical centre and walk along the narrow medieval streets, the sensation becomes a certainty. Tuscany has defi-nitely accustomed us to the beauty of its villages, but Montalcino still conserves a pride and nobility that make it a truly singular town.

The birth of the inhabited centre goes back to the Etruscan and Roman period, as is testified to by the numerous archaeological discoveries in the area, even if the first definite recorded date is in 814 A.D., the year when the act was drawn up with which Ludovico the Pious granted the friar Saint Antimo the land located *"under Mount Lucini"*.

The current urban configuration, in any case, originates around the year 1000, with the settle-ment of refugees from the maremman town of Roselle, who had fled the incursions of Sara-cen pirates.

In the fourteenth century Montalcino was laid out much as it is today, with the exception of the new urban settlements that have been created outside the walls during the last few decades.

Between the twelfth and thirteenth centuries, the destiny of the village went hand in hand with the fortunes of the city of Siena, which saw in Montalcino the ideal strategic position from which to block the expansionistic aims of Florence, which terminated following the historical battle of Montaperti, in which Siena prevailed.

164 - Montalcino, Civic and Diocese Museum of Sacred Art, Master of Saint Catherine of Alexandria (Sienese sculptor early fifteenth century), 'Announcement of the Virgin'

The arts and crafts flowered in the town and the village definitively became a city in the fourteenth century, a fact that was officially sanctioned in 1462 by a Papal Bull of Pope Pius II.

Following the fall of Siena in 1555, the exiles from the city of the Palio retreated to these hillside strongholds, proclaiming the Republic of Siena in Montalcino. The development of the city's monuments took place within the ancient walls, which permit access to the historical centre through five gates: **Cassero gate**, **Burelli gate**, **Castellana gate**, **Gattoli gate** and **Cerbaia gate**.

The Fortress, which dates back to 1362, is located at the

165 - Montalcino, City Hall (or Pori Palace) and Burelli gate

166 - Montalcino, Museo Civic and Diocese Museum of Sacred Art, onyx coat of arms of Montalcino, fourteenth century

entrance to the town. It is a pentagon-shaped rock that dominates the town with its great size; in its long history, the rock has sustained many seiges, but has never been conquered. Access to the large court is through the main gate, which is surmounted by a Sienese arch, which bears the black and white symbol of Siena. Numerous towers rise around the walls and medieval burg, which bear names inspired by the sacred and the profane.

The twelfth century **city hall** is worthy of note. It is today the seat of the City Administration, the Tourist Promotion Company and the Brunello Protection Consortium. Other important constructions are located all round this turreted palace, the symbol of layman power over these lands, such as the **theatre of the Astrusi**, which already existed in the sixteenth century and the **loggia**, two stone arches dating back to the fourteenth century that face the central square.

The testimony of religious worship is consistent.

The thirteenth century **Church of Saint Augustine** has an austere façade with a majestic portal

167 - Montalcino, Church of Saint Augustine, the rose window and portal

168 - Montalcino, panorama of centre

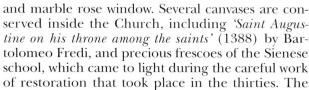

169 - Montalcino, Civic ➡
and Diocese Museum
of sacred art

170 and 171 - Montalcino,
Church of the Virgin of Succour
and Cassero gate

and marble rose window. Several canvases are conserved inside the Church, including *'Saint Augustine on his throne among the saints'* (1388) by Bartolomeo Fredi, and precious frescoes of the Sienese school, which came to light during the careful work of restoration that took place in the thirties. The adjacent Augustinian convent has two sixteenth century cloisters. The entire structure is today the extremely beautiful seat of the **Civic and Diocese Museum of sacred art**.

The **Church of Saint Egidio**, also known as the Church of the Sienese, was the official church of the Republic of Siena in Montalcino. Originally built on the land where a fortress has been erected, it was demolished and rebuilt in 1325 in its current position. A seal of the Republic of Siena is conserved on the portal and, inside the church, there is a collection of flags donated in 1982 by the contrade of the Palio of Siena.

The **Sanctuary of Our Lady of Succour** is very dear to the 'Ilcinese'. It was built in the place where the ancient **gate of Corniolo** was located. In ancient times a table was venerated in this place, which illustrated the Virgin and which is now imbedded in the main altar. There are two interesting canvases in the church: the *'Assumption'* by Vincenzo Tamagni and the *'Calvary'* by Francesco Vanni.

In the highest part of the city the ancient **parish of San Salvatore** rises. It was chosen as a cathedral in 1462 by Pious II and rebuilt in the nineteenth century in neoclassical style, by the Sienese architect Agostino Fantastici. The tufa remains of the ancient portal of the Romanic parish, which are joined by a wall of the baptistery, are interesting, as they date back to the second half of the eleventh century and represent Christ in the mandorla between two angels. The two canvases by Francesco Vanni, painted in his youth, *'Immaculate Conception with Jesus and God the Father'* (1588) and *'Saint John the Baptist in the desert'*.

On one of the sides of Cavour Square an important complex of buildings reveals itself, once the headquarters of the **Our Lady of the Cross hospital**, going back to 1214. The structure, which brought together the seven little hospitals present at that time at Montalcino, has undergone numerous changes down the centuries. Today it is the prestigious headquarters of the town hall and library.

On the right hand side of the building, behind a wrought iron window, we find a small restored area, today intelligently brought to the fore by the local community administration, who has given access to the public. The room entitled 'the writer's desk', was in the beginning a pilgrimage and then the hospital's pharmacy, to then become the administrative headquarters, a place delegated to the drawing up of

172 - Montalcino, Our Lady of the Cross hospital, room 'the writer's desk', fresco detail, Vincenzo Tamagni

173 - Montalcino, Cathedral, ancient parish portal

acts and public documents as well as private transactions. The main feature of the study is that it has been entirely decorated by Vincenzo Tamagni (San Gimignano, 1492-1530), artist of grand expression active at Montalcino, student of Sodoma and collaborator of Raffaello Sanzio during the works of the Vatican loggia.

Illustrious men and heroines are illustrated on the walls (Aristotele, Cicero, Lucrecia, Plato e Scipione), biblical characters (David, Joshua e Giuditta) and more articulate scenes such as the *'Madonna enthroned with child, angels, Saint Girolamo and Saint Augustine'* and *'Our lady of the Cross'*. The presence of designs depicting books and inkwells is also significant, further confirmation of the designated use of the site.

Nowadays, Montalcino hospital is annexed to the **Convent of Saint Francis**, while the nearby church of the same name has been prepared as auditorium.

In two small rooms near the sacristy, several interesting frescoes by Tamagni are conserved: *'Stories from the life of the Virgin'*, *'Domine quo vadis?'* and the *'Fall of the wizard Simon'*.

The **Prison Chapel** should be mentioned, which is located inside the city hall, the **conservatory of Saint Catherine**, which today hosts several schools and the **Church of Saint Mary of Grace**, which is today in a serious state of abandonment.

Just outside the township of Montalcino, in a lovely sunny position among the cypress trees that grow there, we can find the beautiful and historic **Convent of the Observance** building, with the lovely **Nativity of Mary Church**, with its sixteenth century painted portrait of the *'Pietà'*, by Marco Bigio.

175 - Montalcino, Burelli gate

176 - Montalcino,
Convent of the Observance

CIVIC AND DIOCESE MUSEUM OF SACRED ART

177 - 'Virgin with Child, the Redeemer blessing Saints Peter and Paul' by Benvenuto di Giovanni (Siena, 1436-1518?)

Montalcino is a city of art, a town that guards inestimable treasures. One of these is doubtlessly the Civic and Diocese Museum of Sacred Art. Located in the convent of Saint Augustine near the church of the same name, it is characterised by the beauty of the installations and the absolute value of the works exhibited, part of which come from the churches and monasteries located in the city limits of Montalcino. The collection, except for a painted cross (twelfth century), a rare specimen in the Sienese area, from the Abbacy of Sant'Antimo, includes a large collection of Sienese paintings from the period between the fourteenth and fifteenth century, which permits us to enjoy an almost complete panorama of the artists who have made the artistic production of this city great. Objects attributed

178 - 'Bible', 12ᵗʰ century

179 - 'Virgin of Humility', Sano di Pietro (Siena 1406-1481)

to the bottega of Duccio in Segna di Bonaventura are integrated with works by Simone Martini and Ambrogio Lorenzetti, Luca Tommè and Bartolo di Fredi. Even the late gothic season is well represented with the precious works of Giovanni di Paolo and Sano di Pietro. The new Rennaissance season is expressed with a *'Majesty'* by Lorenzo di Pietro, known as the Vecchietta, in the *'Virgin of Mercy'* by Vincenzo Tamagni and in a great panel with the *'Virgin with Child and Saints'*, by Marco Pino. One of the merits of the museum of Montalcino is that it conserves a great collection of painted wooden sculpture: the decisive and expressive style of Giovanni Pisano offers visitors a *'Virgin with Child'*; a small *'Crucifixion'* with elegant lines, which is attributed to Giovanni d'Agostino, the great sculptor and architect of the new Duomo of Siena, who understood how to translate the elaborate depictions of Simone Martini in sculpture. Additionally, the two groups of the Annunciation and several *'Crucifixions'* document the high level of technical ability attained by the Sienese masters in the second half of the fourteenth century. The great age of late gothic culture is instead represented by a *'Saint John the Baptist'* by the Sienese goldsmith-sculptor Giovanni di Turino, a convinced admirer of the 'manner' of the Florentine artist Lorenzo Ghiberti, and by two in-laid figures by Francesco di Valdambrino: an imposing *'San*

180 - 'Angel chandelier holder', Sienese production, seventeenth century

181 - 'Announced Virgin', Domenico di Agostino?, (Siena, documented from 1343 to 1367)

Pietro' donated to Montalcino by Pope Pious III and a *'Crucifixion'*, which marks the apex of this gentile and refined Sienese sculptor, a friend and collaborator of Jacopo della Quercia. The glass-veined earthenware vessels created by Andrea Della Robbia are also very beautiful. The museum also conserves two volumes of a finely illuminated Bible (twelfth century), a *'Crucifix'* of the late sixteenth century by Gianbologna and an exceptional collection, the only one of its kind in Italy, of 52 majolica goblets, produced locally between the end of the

183 - *'Polypty
of Coronation of
the Virgin'*, Bartolo
di Fredi (Siena,
documented
from 1353-died
in 1410)

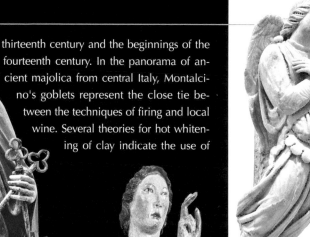

thirteenth century and the beginnings of the fourteenth century. In the panorama of ancient majolica from central Italy, Montalcino's goblets represent the close tie between the techniques of firing and local wine. Several theories for hot whitening of clay indicate the use of

186 - 'Adoring angel', Sienese sculptor, fifteenth century

185 - 'Saint Peter', Francesco di Valdambrino (Siena, documented from 1401 to 1435)

residual dregs from vinification in the firing process as one of the most efficient ways to obtain certain chromatic effects, and this is one of the many testimonies of the importance of vine growing in this territory, during every age of its history.

186 - 'Announcing angel', Angelo di Nalduccio (late fourteenth century painter and sculptor)

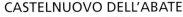

188 - Castelnuovo dell'Abate,
Velona Castle

189 - Castelnuovo dell'Abate,
the tufa mine (also called
the 'onyx' or 'alabaster' mine)
utilised for construction
of the Sant'Antimo abbacy

CASTELNUOVO DELL'ABATE

Castelnuovo dell'Abate rises on the top of a hill, as a bastion of the roads that climb up from the Orcia Valley and the ancient footpaths of Mount Amiata. The village developed around the year 1000, thanks to the activity of the monks in the nearby Sant'Antimo Abbacy. The friars lived in a castle, of which there remains today only a gate, and the village takes its name from their presence. The village, in any case, was built over a pre-existing Roman settlement, whose traces are still evident today throughout the area.

The Sienese fortified the burg after having extended their hegemony throughout the countryside, making it the border stronghold of the Orcia River. It is a pleasant village to visit. The ancient gate, tracts of the original wall and the seventeenth century **bishopric** are admirable. They were built by Fabius De Vecchis, bishop of Montalcino, and later purchased by the Piccolomini family, where Enea Silvio was born – better known as Pope Pious II.

The **parish of Saints Phillip and James**, which has two interesting sixteenth century frescoes by Ventura Salimbeni, is located in the centre of the village. Not far away from the centre, in the direction of Mount Amiata, stands the privately owned **Castle of the Velona**, dominating the Orcia Valley, which can be reached from an unpaved road.

Today it is a prestigious hotel and the complex is made up of two towered buildings, connected by other lower sections, modified with respect to the original construction by restoration that took place in the nineteenth century.

From the courtyard of the castle, the **Chapel of San Biagio** can be reached. The painting by Benvenuto di Giovanni, entitled '*Virgin with Child and Saints Biagio and Bartholomew*' was originally located in this chapel, and is today conserved at the National Gallery in Urbino, while a copy is conserved in the Museum of Montalcino.

The locality of Sesta is included in the territory of this suburb. The seventeenth century **chapel of Saint Catherine of Siena** is located in Sesta. Saint Catherine is also known by the name Saint Petronilla.

At the bottom of the hill, we find a pearl of Tuscan Romanic architecture, the **Abbacy of Sant'Antimo**. The archaeological findings, which go back to extremely ancient times, long before the birth of Christ, witness human settlements that indicate that the area has long been considered a sacred site. It is a well-known fact that the main Christian Churches were prevalently built on sites that had been used for previous religious worship. The complex seems to have been spared the structural crisis experienced by other important religious sites in the area, which have left only suggestive ruins, such as the nearby San Galgano.

There is still life today in the Abbacy of Sant'Antimo, one of the dearest places for Tuscans, religious and scholars throughout Christianity. Millions of tourists, summer and winter, climb through these hills to admire and photograph this architectural wonder and its pleasant surroundings from every angle, where olive trees over a thousand years old still thrive.

190 - Castelnuovo dell'Abate, abbacy of Sant'Antimo, double lancet window on façade

THE ABBACY OF SANT'ANTIMO

The Abbacy of Sant'Antimo, built according to the canons of Benedictine tradition, is definitely the most important Romanic monument in southern Tuscany. It has a structure inspired by French architectural modules, especially in the basilica plant and the walkway with radial chapels, typical of the great medieval churches of pilgrimage.

191 - high relief, detail of façade

192 - apse

193 - the abbacy among olive orchards

194 and 195 - figures outside the abbacy

The close ties with Cluniac culture is evident in the soaring perspective of the central nave. The workers who built it were probably Lombard, but the style is evidently greatly influenced by the French school. This can be interpreted from the columns interrupted by cross-shaped pillars, and the presence of depictions of gryphons, eagles and dragons. The capitals, and their origin, is instead something that has been discussed widely, but examination of the refined sculpted motifs has convinced many experts that the work was supervised by Frenchmen. The natural seat hosting the Abbacy presents geographical and landscape characteristics that strongly distinguish it from

any other abbacy in a range of many kilometers. Located in a narrow valley protected on three sides by the high hills of the Ilcinese plateau, dense with perfumed and bright Mediterranean vegetation, the abbacy rises, of unusual size with respect to other rural parishes in the area, at the end of the only road of access from Montalcino. History recounts that the original abbacy was built by Carlo Magno in the ninth century. Among the many works of art in the church, the

sculpted group in painted wood depicting the *'Virgin on her throne with Child'* (1260), the twelfth century *'Crucifixion'* in inlaid and painted wood, the splendid capital of the second column on the right, attributed to the Master of Cabstany, which reproduces a series of lions, and the fifteenth century escoes depicting the *'Eight stories from the life of Saint Benedict'*, are worthy of mention.

196 - the facade with a millenary olive tree

197 - 'Mary with the Evangelists', 16th century, high relief of the facade

198 - high relief of the facade

➡ 199 - Castelnuovo dell'Abate, nocturnal view of the abbacy of Sant'Antimo

SANT'ANGELO IN COLLE

As we enter the second fork of the road from Montalcino, we come to Sant'Angelo in Colle, a small fortified burg of great beauty, which overlooks the surrounding area in all directions from its perch at 500 m a.s.l.

The village is a veritable architectural jewel, dominated at its gate by an enormous tower known as 'il Cassero', and built along a series of concentric roads like spokes, with the main church and palaces of the notables in the centre. Surrounded by walls and pensile gardens, Sant'Angelo was mentioned as early as 715, in a description of the local clergyman by the Lombard Allerat, for the benefit of the Legate of the Lombard King Liutprando. Later the village came under the influence of the Sienese, who obtained its submission after long and arduous battle. From the peak of Siena's towers, towards the end of the century, the Ghibellines took refuge here and the Hospital of Saint Mary della Scala, which is today the seat of an important civic museum, built one of its farms in Sant'Angelo.

The ancient village is still perfectly conserved and splendidly maintained today by the inhabitants, and represents an oasis of peace for travellers, submerged in the vastness of the surrounding valleys. The main square is dominated by the Romanic Church, the **parish of the Archangel St. Michael**. Other monuments present among the small, terraced medieval homes include the **Church of the Virgin of Mercy**, with a fresco of the *'Resurrection of Christ'* and a wooden cross, and the **Church of St. Peter**.

There is written testimony, at the State Archives of Siena, left by Bartolomeo Gherardini, of an inn that was operated in the sixteenth century in Sant'Angelo in Colle, where it appears that wine was sold *"at more than equitable prices"*. It was practically an erstwhile wine shop, another sign of the ante litteram predilection for modernity of this territo-

200 - Sant'Angelo in Colle, wooden statue of Saint Michael, conserved in the church

201 - Sant'Angelo in Colle, characteristic stone house

202 - Sant'Angelo in Colle, panorama

ry. We also learn from the document in question that *"the court of the Castle is small and the soil sterile when it comes to grain, but fruitful in oil and wine, and especially in oil"*. The author then notes that about 700 some of wine are produced in Sant'Angelo, which are sent to the Maremman and Ilcinese markets *"and even to Siena"*.

It may be hypothesized that a soma amounted to about 200 kilos of product, which allow us to understand that as early as the sixteenth century, these lands produced a good 1400 kilos of wine, in addition to what was kept for the consumption of the 'hearth' families, that is to say the landowners who worked here.

CAMIGLIANO

South of Sant'Angelo, perfectly visible from its wall and nestled among the woody hills and protected by vast ravines of sandstone, the last great terrace before the Maremma valleys hosts the small burg of Camigliano, surrounded by vast extensions of vineyards and cultivated land, which was a prehistoric Etruscan settlement. In early medieval times Camigliano probably belonged to the Ardengheschi, until it entered the Sienese orbit in the twelfth century. In 1330 it was destroyed by Pisa and later became a farm of the Hospital of Saint Mary della Scala.

In the 2001 census, this tiny burg had a population of 26. Laid out around the main country house, it was rebuilt over the pre-existent building in the nineteenth century.

The stone houses nestle against each other, leaving room for small squares, gardens, streets and stone passageways. The Roman **parish of Saints Biagio and Donato** stands out with its sculpted figures of ancient sacred symbols on the façade.

The **Archway square** is the heart of the village, with its central **well**, where the most popular village feast takes place, the 'feast of the rooster', which is celebrated at the end of September. Returning towards Montalcino, between the roads of the two castles of Argiano and Camigliano, we come to Tavernelle, a gracious agricultural settlement that overlooks the road that climbs up towards Montalcino from the Maremman villages, after passing the castle of Poggio alle Mura.

TORRENIERI

On the opposite side of Montalcino, Torrenieri, one of the best-known stopovers on the Lucca-Siena-Rome road, spreads out in a direct line along the road. The town's name comes from the first settlement in historical memory, a fortified outpost with a black tower.

It became famous in the diary of travels of the British Bishop Sigeric, who described it as having been a hotel since the year 1000, transformed into a dwelling around the twelfth century. It was then raised to the dignity of a castle and its current name was made official. It is characterised by its position on an obligatory itinerary along the via Francigena.

206 - Torrenieri, old post office

207 - Torrenieri, view

Dante probably stopped in Torrenieri during a trip to Rome and, in the fourteenth century, several events in the town are recounted in the novel of the ninth day of the Decameron, by Giovanni Boccaccio. In the eighteenth century census, Torrenieri was described as follows: *"on the road from Siena to Rome, upon an easily accessible hill, entirely cultivated in vines and olives, the small castle of Torrenieri"*.

Today it is a flowering village between Montalcino and the roadways toward Umbria and Lazio.

Among the works of art that are worth mentioning here in this volume we can really count on the lovely **Church of Saint Mary Magdalene** with its finely made and beautufully presented wooden sculpture of the *'Virgin on her throne with Child'*, by the artist sculptor Domenico di Niccolò dei Cori, dating from between the second and third decades of the fifteenth century. In the nearby sixteenth century **oratory of the Company of Saint Rocco**, frescoes of the same era depict the *'Virgin with Child'*.

208 - Poggio alle Mura, the castle

209 - Romitorio Castles

210 - Argiano Castles

PARISHES AND CASTLES

Among the castles that have remained, which have not become extended villages, Argiano, Castelgiocondo, Castiglion del Bosco, Poggio alle Mura and Romitorio are worthy of mention. They have today become the authoritative home offices of Brunello di Montalcino producers.

The **Castle of Argiano**, located at the end of a vast plateau halfway between Sant'Angelo in Colle and Camigliano, saw its greatest development around the seventeenth century, as witnessed in the notes of the *"most illustrious Lord"* Bartolomeo Gherardini, which contain a compendium of his visit in 1676: *"the holdings of Argiano are very productive in oil, with its beautiful olive plantations"*. The notes also explain that there were 95 sold in Argiano, divided among 16 hearths, and that 100 some of wine were produced; approximately 200 hectolitres.

Gherardini notes that **Poggio alle Mura** produced *"lively wine but not in great quantity"* and that there were 203 inhabitants in 41 hearths. The quantity of wine produced is indicted as 200 some – more or less 40,000 kilos of wine. Poggio alle Mura is currently owned by the Banfi vineyard and is the seat of the museum of glass and crystal. The thirteenth century **parish of San Sigismondo** is located in the vicinity of the castle. The painting by Benvenuto di Giovanni depicting *'San Sigismondo'*, which is today conserved in the Civic and Diocese Museum of sacred art in Montalcino, was originally located in this church.

Almost side-by-side with Montalcino, the square, monumental walls of **Romitorio Castle** rise: the fortress dates from the beginning of the second millennium. It is of classical form, with turrets at each corner and a wall to protect the southern side, which is still extant today and marks of a vast garden area.

Castelgiocondo is about a century older. It is a large structure that was almost entirely rebuilt in the nineteenth century and which includes a tower with embattlements, a valuable church, with the **Chapel of Saint Gerolamo** and the remains of what was once the **parish of Saint Michael**.

Dominating the tract of the Ombrone River Valley north of Montalcino, we find Castiglione del Bosco, a small village located among lush oak woods, at the summit of the high hills surrounding the capital. Here, among streets and small, precious palaces of more recent construction, we can admire the ruins of the **medieval castle** and the **Church of Saint Michael**.

The **Abbey of Ardenga** is a religious complex that governed vast agricultural holdings, starting from the Middle Ages, along the road from Montalcino to Torrenieri. Today we can admire the *loggia*, the *portico*, the *abbey crypt of Saint Andrew the*

211 - Benvenuto di Giovanni (Siena, 1436-1518?), *'San Sigismondo'*. Work from the parish of San Sigismondo, now exhibited at the Civic and Diocese Museum of Sacred Art of Montalcino

Apostle and the *portal* with the coat of arms of the Ardenghi, the noble family that gave its name to the locality.

The **Parish of Saint Restituta** is located in an intermediate and lovely position, protected by the castles and the Poggio Civitella. It was constructed in the fourteenth century over what was once a Roman settlement, but we can note here that there are even more ancient and historic settlements in the immediate vicinity. An old roadway that harks back to the ancient splendour of the Etruscan peoples gradually winds its way in an easterly direction, some sections still being identifiable, and the age-old tombs by the country roadside are not so rare, although they have long been empty now, and were often used as deposits for bottles.

212 - Parish of Saint Restituta

213 - Ardenga Abbacy

Typical products and cuisine

An itinerary and overview of agricultural and foodstuffs products, local cuisine and a menu with Brunello as an ingredient of dishes prepared by eight restaurants

8

214 - Tuscan salami

215 - hams in the process of salting

Typical products and cuisine

216 - pore mushrooms

ILCINESE CUISINE

The local cuisine in this area reflects the sobre but at the same time 'happy' cuisine of the Tuscan people. The main recipes are based on several select ingredients: extra virgin olive oil, goat's milk or sheep's milk cheese from the Sienese crete area, sweets, honey, San Giovanni d'Asso and Asciano truffles, mushrooms, Amiata chestnuts, salami and meats.

There are therefore not a great number of elements that make up Ilcinese cuisine, which uses the spit and grate more than in other places, to obtain light, lean and savoury meat dishes; there is a constant and fundamental presence of oil, vegetables and unsalted bread, which are at the base of traditional Sienese soups.

It is a cuisine that represents one of the tastiest examples of the mediterranean diet, which makes extensive use of savoury herbs, gathered wild from the lush vegetation around the capital town, the burgs and suburbs, and which also utilises garlic, onions, celery and scallion.

This cuisine makes traditional use of wild game, while among the winter soups, the 'ribollita' has dominated traditional soups for centuries. It is a bean soup, which is left to cool after cooked and then reheated again with the addition of oil. Among the typical dishes is 'pinci', a Sienese version of hand-drawn spaghetti, dressed with meat and tomato sauce, with plenty of garlic and breadcrumbs (grated bread fried in oil).

The tradition of the Chianine steak cooked on hot coals without a flame can certainly not be neglected. These are typical, simple dishes, after which it is appropriate to wind up the meal with a good selection of sweets.

Finally, the taste of these full, elegant and harmonious wines precisely reflect the character of the hills from which the grapes originate, which are used in their production.

217 - a dish of pinci

EXTRA VIRGIN OLIVE OIL

Extra virgin olive oil is obtained from grinding Montalcino olives and definitely, second only to the wine, it is the most typical product of these hills. History, recorded in the chronicles of time, takes us back to the farms and castles of Montalcino, as early as the year 1000, when the production of olive oil was of equal importance, if not greater, than the production of wine.

In our own day, the local landscapes with olive groves are very suggestive, the high reigns upon the summit of certain hills, where the silhouettes of olive trees stand out against the sky, olive trees that have resisted the freezing winters of ages past. Or, in the vicinity of the Abbacy of Sant'Antimo, where enormous contorted and twisted trunks more than a thousand years old allow us to understand how much human and even natural history has passed underneath the branches, of an almost metallic green colour, of this great patriarch of nature.

The more protected areas of the Ilcinese territory are still rich in these ancient and majestic olive groves, from which a dense and spicy oil is still obtained.

In effect, we are dealing with the purest species, in genetical terms, which was born as it is and has not undergone crossing or cloning, but has always been inserted in the local landscape. The olives produced are small, numerous, of several tones of green and with smoke-black shading. The

218 - old tools for the conservation of olives

production of oil rarely reaches high levels, but the product retains its fine, ancient and original taste.

Alongside these older olive groves, there are also new plantations today, most of which were planted after the great freezing of 1985, which distroyed most of the patrimony of olive plantations in Tuscany.

The other different olive species that can be found in these hills are the ones which are also traditionally planted elsewhere in the region: the moraiolo, which provides small, round kernels of a marked brownish colour, and the leccino, which is reminiscent in its development of the emblematic tree of the locality.

The activity of the small olive presses, often found at olive growers' farms themselves, ceased their work long ago, in favour of the collective high technology presses for extraction of the oil. The machinery that once used animal power, such as donkeys, until a few decades ago, was later equipped with electric motors. Montalcino was actually the first town in the area to get electric energy, even before Siena itself. The olives, of course, must be healthy and clean and, above all, pressed the same day they are gathered, to avoid problems that

219 - olives at harvest

220 - old olive tree

could develop in the taste of the oil due to mould or other pathologies. More recently, following the development that the image of extra virgin olive oil has undergone in recent years, many experiments have been conducted in the pressing of olives, utilising only one species, to obtain only oil of oleaster, moraiolo or pendolino olives.

The results in the final analysis in these pressing experiments after taking all things into consideration have permitted a notable amplification in terms of the range of taste of the product, exalting the characteristics of either one or the other of the differeing classifications or types of the olives.

This honest and beneficial oil is used to prepare the principal gastronomical recipes of local tradition.

221 - extra virgin olive oil

222 - old olive press

THE HONEY

Apiculture is an art that is highly appraised in this area. The honey obtained is typical inasmuch as the vast extension of mediterranean vegetation and woods makes this an area where beekeepers position their apiaries.

A wildflower product is thus obtained that bears the essences of genista, wild rose, strawberry and even chestnut in its organoleptic base; when it isn't actually 'apple-scented', which can even happen – it is a dense and soft honey, created by the honey-collecting bees in the woods, which is seasonally offered to the palate and senses of connoisseurs.

Current trends of local restaurant keepers have made honey part of the menu, to accompany other typical local products, such as the goat's milk cheese.

223 - honey

224 - honey combined with Tuscan goat's and sheep's milk cheeses

THE CHEESES

Few herds have remained, but in the past, when it was time for transhumances, the area was crowded with them, and pastures and fodder stocks witnessed the passage and sojourn of sheep and cattle, whose milk was transformed into the perfumed dairy products characteristic of the area. But sheep's and goat's milk cheese still has a great deal of productive potential, thanks to the fact that the area is in the vicinity of one of the richest dairy zones in Italy, the Pienza area, which has based its rural economy on this product.

We have left the vast wild hills of underbrush, dominated by the Sienese crete, which extend in every direction from the base of the Ilcinese hills – an ideal terrain for raising sheep and goats; but the tradition of producing the best known types of goat's and sheep's milk cheese, sweet or salted, fresh, semi-seasoned or aged, is still solidly anchored in the hands of a few local experts. Goat's milk cheese is quite suitable, sweetened with honey, to accompany the sweet wines produced in this area – Moscadello or Vin Santo, but it is also exquisite when it accompanies some of the more structured red wines.

The success and notoriety of this cheese, which has a semi-hard consistency, derives from the combination of two overlaying pastoral cultures: the local one and the Sardinian one, which substituted the extensive cultivations of the Sienese lands with its herds in the fifties

225 - sheep's milk cheese

of the last century. The Sienese lands had long been abandoned, left uncultivated and transformed into vast pastures suitable for cattle. They were poor pastures, due to the lack of rain in the area, but were extremely rich as far as the quality of the tasty, dense grass, full of nutritional substances was concerned.

It is this perfumed and tasty grass that confers the special taste upon the milk of the sheep, and it is not rare, alonside the herds of sheep, to see small groups of goats, whose milk, which is less fat and finer than sheep's milk, is formed from a diet that also takes advantage of the underbrush and bark of the mediterranean vegetation, which is so abundant here. Small quantities of goat's milk are often present in the milk destined for the production of Tuscan sheep's milk cheese.

In the event the cheese is to be consumed fresh, the curds, that is to say the mass in which the milk is coagulated, is broken into a certain grade dimension, while if it is for aging, the curds are broken into smaller lumps.

226 - sheep

227, 228, 229 and 230 - several cheeses produced at the Barbi Farm: Wine 'cacio', peppered 'cacio' cheese, fresh sheep's milk cheese and season goat's milk cheese in nut leaves

THE CURING OF PORK

The hunting of wild boar, which has taken place in this area since the most distant past and which once guaranteed the food supply of much of the local population, is the base from which the art of pork butchering and the processing of pork meats has developed in Montalcino.

231 and 232 - swines

From wild boar to the authothonous species such as the Sienese country boar, and in more recent times the white species, which has a greater productive yield, the step was short and was faced with ability by most of the artisans in the capital and its suburbs.

From the muscular backs of the wild boar and Sienese country boar come strings of dark, compact sausages and roughly

flavoured ham. While the white meats of the modern species provide, in addition to loin of pork, steaks and ribs to be roasted over the coals, which they call 'costoleccio' here, as well as fresh sausages and perfumed salamis, aromatic 'finocchiona' cured meat and soppressa sausages.

Finocchiona is a preparation of fat and lean fresh pork, aromatised with fennel seeds, which is very typical of the area of Florence. Soppressa, on the other hand is a rough butchering of all of the soft parts of the head, which is pressed in a cloth after prolonged boiling. It is not rare to find lovers of 'the good things of old times'. It is a bit more rare, on the other hand, to find people like Carlo Pieri, who has made this passion a winning economic enterprise.

The rigorous selection of the animals to send to slaughter and the use of traditional techniques, in full respect of modern health standards, make his 'bottega' one of the most widely known and appraised in the area.

Carlo Pieri and his dynamic wife express themselves best in the art of processing pork, with a series of refined preparations that make their typical nature the primary value.

The raw material comes directly from their farm, where the animals are raised in respect of

233 and 234 - coats of arms with a Sienese Cinta boar

235 - hams

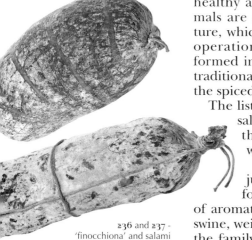

healthy and natural nutritional values. The animals are slaughtered in a modern private structure, which the family manages themselves, in co-operation with other pork farmers, and transformed into ham, various salamis, hams and cuts, traditional and soppressa sausages, obtained from the spiced innards of the swine.

The list of bacon and rolled meats, finocchiona, salted cheek, blood sausage, loin and liver, the latter treated with salt, pepper and wild fennel seeds just goes on and on.

Their traditional 'porchetta', finally, just cannot be missed. It is cooked slowly for hours and hours with a secret mixture of aromatic herbs. Porchetta is an entire yearling swine, weighing no more than 20 kilos, taken from the family stock, where the maximum number of animals to be fattened never exceeds 200 swine and where the cycle of quality is ensured with total control, including the butchering operations themselves.

236 and 237 -
'finocchiona' and salami

238 - 'porchetta'

239 - Carlo Pieri at work ➡
in his butcher shop

SIENESE CRETE TRUFFLES

Truffles are a type of mushroom that grow underground, like a tuber. They have a meaty mass, called the 'glebe', covered by a sort of bark, known as the 'peridium'. The 'white truffle of Crete', one of the most renowned italian truffles and, consequently, one of the most renowned in the world, is worked with mastery and love, thanks to the industrious activity of the Truffle Producers' Association. The free time of these amateurs is often dedicated to preserving the state of the truffle grounds, a reserve that extends for more than 40 hectares around San Giovanni d'Asso.

Cleaning ditches and maintaining the compactness of the terrain are part of this activity, to ensure that the magnatum pyco is renewed at the end of the summer, which is the ideal habitat for the spontaneous growth of truffles.

The truffle is made of a high percentage of water and mineral salts, absorbed by the ground through the roots of the tree where truffles live in symbiosis. In fact, truffles are born and grow near the roots of trees, especially poplars, linden or basswood, oak and willows, becoming a veritable parasite.

The characteristics of colour, taste and perfume of truffles are determined by the type of tree they develop in the vicinity of. Oak truffles have a stronger perfume, while the ones that grow near linden trees are lighter in colour and aromatic. The shape, on the other hand, depends on the type of terrain. If the terrain is soft the truffles will be smoother. If it is compact, it will present nodules and outgrowths, because of the difficulty it encounters in creating a space for itself.

240 and 241 - Sienese Crete truffle and 'tagliolini' pasta with truffles

THE PINCI

Accompanied by wild game sauce, pasta is always present in the local gastronomical tradition. It can be consumed as a first course, before a dish of thrush, roasted or cooked on a spit (which are considered a delicacy if eaten without cleaning out the innards). One of the most characteristic and traditional local pasta dishes for a great first course is the hard grain pinci pasta, a large spaghetti made by hand, which is only cooked fresh. Pinci (which the Sienese have called instead Pici), is the most common and characteristic dish found on local restaurant menus, because it is the restaurant who are the true interpreters of the traditional Ilcinese cuisine.

Cooked in salty boiling water and drained, the Pinci may be dressed in a variety of ways. In Montalcino the most typical preparations are with meat sauce or 'with crumbs'. The latter being nothing more than Tuscan bread crust crumbs, cooked in olive oil with garlic, salt and pepper.

242 - preparing pinci

TAGLIOLI AL BRUNELLO WITH VEGETABLE RAGOUT

INGREDIENTS FOR 4 SERVINGS
400 g of taglioli al Brunello, extra virgin olive oil, salt, 100 g of peas, 2 potatoes, 1 carrot, 1 pepperoni, 1 zucchini squash, 5 white asparagus, hot pepper, fresh Pienza sheep's milk cheese, saffron, vegetable broth

Clean and wash the greens carefully, cut them julienne style and cook them in a casserole with a bit of oil, a pinch of hot pepper and little salt. Cook the taglioli in an abundant pan of boiling salted water, drain them and pan fry quickly with the vegetable ragout. In the meantime prepare the broth and saffron with the mashed potatoes in a dense cream and serve on a bed of taglioli. Add a sprinkling of grated sheep's milk cheese.

244 - 'taglioli al Brunello' of the 'Club del Naturista'

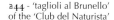

TAGLIOLI AL BRUNELLO

Alongside this traditional dish, it is in any case possible to find several other peculiar pasta dishes, which are the fruit of local fantasy and intuition. Among these, it is impossible to forget the particular proposal of Antonio and Maria Laura Pignatello, the owners of the 'Club del Naturista', a Pienza firm specialised in marketing quality biological products with the AIAB certification.

In addition to their rich array of products, such as honey, biscuits and several non-alcoholic digestive liqueurs, which are produced with rhubarb and a knowing mix of herbs, these two entrepeneurs, whose desire it is to protect biological production, have decided to market a special pasta, which they have called 'taglioli al Brunello'. This wonderful invention of theirs is riding the wave of the success of the famous wine.

Taglioli al Brunello pasta is prepared with hard grain semola, eggs and 5 per cent of Brunello di Montalcino, which gives them their characteristic colour and taste. The pasta is then drawn through brass, cut patiently by hand and dried on straw, where it rests for at least 12 hours, with the assistance of moderate heating.

245, 246, 247, 248 and 249 - typical Montalcino sweets: 'panforte' and 'panforte nero', 'morselletti', 'brutti ma buoni' ('ugly but tasty') and 'cantucci' biscuits

SWEETS AND PASTRY

The gastronomical invention of local artisans is shown best in the art of pastry.

In addition to the cakes tied to particular times of the year, such as the sophisticated 'crogetti', traditional carnival shakes of a very thin puff pastry, or 'dead bones', which have a disquieting name but also an incomparable fragrance, 'morselletti' are baked daily in Montalcino. These are a sort of extremely soft almond pastry, then there are the 'ugly but tasty' shots of meringue that cover dry fruit, the 'tegole' and 'sospiri', dry biscuits and flakes of sugared egg white.

The vicinity to Siena, inevitably, has made it a tradition to produce 'panforte' which is prepared in the classical and 'black' versions, enriched with chocolate.

At the end of the parade of typical sweets are the 'migliaccio' and 'donzelle'.

OVERCOOKED WILD BOAR

INGREDIENTS FOR 8 SERVINGS
2 kg of leg of boar, 2 glasses of extra virgin olive oil, 250 g of bacon, 2 bay leaves, 2 red onions, 2 cloves of garlic, 2 carrots, meat broth, 150 g of pulped tomatoes, 2 litres of well-bodied red wine, 3 glasses of vinegar, parsley, thyme, 3 spikes of cloves, grain pepper, salt, pepper

Prepare the marination with wine, vinegar, the onions, the carrots, the grain pepper, the parsley, the thyme and the cloves, all minced. Let it boil over a low flame for 30 minutes. Cool and add to glasses of oil. Cover the meat well with this sauce and allow it to marinate completely for one whole day. Very lightly fry minced celery, bacon, garlic and onion, add the bay leaves and add the meat, cut into pieces. Let it brown, cover with the marinated sauce, continue cooking over a low flame, until the sauce evaporates. Add the tomatoes and continue cooking, adding a dipper of boiling broth periodically. When done make savoury with a small amount of minced capers, salt and pepper.

WILD GAME

The vast terrain of the ancient noble families of southern Tuscany were once managed as plantation estates.

The environmental impact provoked by the agronomic systems was almost nil and this element, together with the prohibition to hunt and the vastity of the natural area, favoured the presence of numerous species of wild game, both indigenous and non indigenous, such as the rabbit, the pheasant, the partridge, various hoofed animals and birds, including the wild dove, thrush and woodcocks.

The territory of the land holdings was defended by armed guards, who tried to impede poaching. Later a set of regulations was promulgated to favour the turnover of wild species.

Today it has become extremely difficult to come into the possession of a wild animal to prepare according to the traditional recipes, for those who do not like to carry a rifle and go hunting. Therefore, a meal with spitted thrush, leper in salmì

251 - game

sauce or stuffed partridge, or the possibility of tasting the savoury meat of the woodcock, is an event that one should remember for a long time.

252 - grappa tasting

253 - the grappa salesman in a nineteenth century print

BRUNELLO GRAPPA

Grappa was considered a humble beverage for a long time, suitable to perk up sad spirits or pick oneself up from hard winter days, in uncomfortable or unpleasant situations. Only in recent years has it finally been appropriately recognised by the most refined palates, and represents one of the most original products of distilling art.

In Montalcino many firms transform their best marc into grappa, to complete the range of company products. Sangiovese marc, after soft pressing, is sent to the distillery while they are still humid, which extracts a clear and potent liquid, which is good for consumption or for aging in durmast casks.

It has a characteristic taste, is extremely strong for the taste of smell, but is perfumed and penetrating. The peculiarity of Brunello grappa is its high level of alcohol content, which is softened by the floreal aromas of the Sangiovese marc, in some cases to the point that it assumes an almost feminine sweetness.

To best appreciate the characteristics of this product, it is served best at 10-15° C, if it is a young distilled product, and at 17-20° C if it is aged. The glass to use should be small, of the characteristic tulip shape, which permits the slow and progressive release of the aromas.

Upon tasting, the first sip should be distributed all over the palate, giving a pleasant and sweet after taste, that mitigates the violence of the impact with the alcohol.

ORCIA VALLEY SAFFRON

Saffron has been known in Italy since Roman times, when it was used to cook wild game and to prepare aromatic wines.

Ovidio said that the name was derived from Crocus, an Indo-European pastor who, desperate in seeing young Smirax die of love for him, asked Zeus to be able to hold wake over the remains of his loved one, in the form of a flower. In ancient Greece, it was used as a spice to aromatise foods, for its ability to enhance good humour and sexual performance, as a colouring for cloth and a funda-

254 - the separation of the saffron stigma from *Crocus* flowers

mental element for the best perfumes. In Greek mythology it possessed a heroic value: the god Hermes, counsellor of lovers, reawoke sexual desire with this spice. In Persia it was also widely used as an aphrodisiac.

Later, in medieval times, it became the symbol of wealth. Just imagine that 50 grams of this unmistakeable red powder, with its inebriating aroma, was worth the price of a horse.

In the thirteenth century it was the most widely known and highly appraised plant in the Sienese territory and was considered to be precious, as it constituted a veritable source of wealth for those who cultivated it. The academic Antonio Targioni Tozzetti (1785-1856), in his course of botanic medicine and pharmacy, stated that the crocus *"grows in areas of Siena and was much cultivated in the sixteenth century as a precious plant"*.

In the centuries the tradition of cultivating the plant has been lost. Nevertheless, there are sufficient historical elements to speak of the Orcia Valley as one of the areas where it was cultivated. In the territory of Asciano, Montalcino and San Quirico, in several contracts for sharecroppers, saffron appears as part of the rent of the sharecroppers, who made a commitment, under penalty of resolution of the contract, to plant a certain established amount of saffron.

The characteristic basis that distinguishes the good quality of the saffron is the power colorant, that in a product of high quality should never be less than 200mgs per kilogram.

The spice we use for the unmistakeable and delicate taste of many dishes is non other than the pistil of the flower Crocus Sativus, which is part of the family of the Iridacee, with lance-shaped leaves and a violate, lone flower, which flowers in autumn.

MONTALCINO TRIPE

INGREDIENTS FOR 4 SERVINGS
800 g boiled veal tripe, 0.25 g of pure saffron, 1 white onion, 1 clove of garlic, 150 g extra virgin olive oil, 100 g of grated cheese, 1 cup of chicken broth, salt, pepper

Wash the tripe well and carefully cut it into different strips. Prepare a pan carefully with minced onions, garlic and different types of herbs, very slightly fried in olive oil, add the tripe and let it take on the taste, adding a little salt. In the meantime make an infusion of saffron, for one hour, in a glass of luke-warm water. Add it to the tripe together with the broth and cook for 40 minutes, until the cooking sauce appears only slightly liquid. Serve piping hot, covering with pepper and grated cheese.

The Brandi family has continued this tradition today. They have been farmers for many generations, and have always dedicated themselves to this profession with passion and love, attempting to attain the best of saffron production. On a surface of 15.000 m², they get about 13 kilos of the product.

This order of measurement may seem scarce if compared to other cultivations, but in reality it isn't. In fact, it must be born in mind that all of the operations must be carried out rigorously by hand, from the harvest to the planting of the bulbs, to gathering the flowers, separating the stigmas, which are the true saffron, from the flowers and packaging. It must therefore be understood that everything requires careful attention and a production time that absolutely cannot be compared to any other type of cultivation.

The Brandis have become fine producers of saffron in the space of a few years. The family is committed in all of the various operations, which are carried out at different times. Planting of the bulbs is done in August, while the flowers are gathered in November. These are all operations that require hard work and care, to ensure the quality of the final product.

256 - *Crocus* in flower

257 - phase of saffron processing

BANFI BALSAMIC PRODUCTION

Grape must does not always end up as wine. Sometimes, and with splendid results for the joy of the palate, it is transformed into balsamic vinegar.

At Montalcino, in the tranquillity of one of the austere and hundred-year old cellars of the Poggio alle Mura castle, part of the Banfi grape harvest of Moscatello and Trebbiano is pressed, filtered and lightly cooked. At a later stage, long ageing transforms the cooked must into the dark, round and fragrant balsam that reminds us of the heritage passed down from the Etruscan gastronomic culture.

This specific balsamic mix is the result of a slow ageing of the cooked must, which is decanted with Botticelle casks, acquiring in transference, over a period of 12 years, the fragrance and character of oak wood, of chestnut, of cherry, of ash wood and of mulberry. The result is a dense liquid, spicy, with a sweet and sour taste, with a light note of acidity, excellent condiment above all for white and red meat, but which does not disdain from being the ingredient for dishes with a pasta base, rice or fruit based dessert.

≥58 - Botticelle casks of Banfi balsamic production

≥59 - Etruscan balsamic sauce

first course

pinci with Brunello ragout sauce

- 600 g of 00 flour
- 1 egg
- corn flour
- salt
- 300 g of minced veal
- 1 kg of minced pork
- 1 onion
- 1 stick of celery
- 1 carrot
- 1 bunch of parsley
- 3 glasses of Brunello di Montalcino docg
- extra virgin olive oil
- water

Prepare the pinci by mixing the flour with the egg, oil, salt and a glass of cold water. When the pasta is homogeneous and smooth, spread it with a rolling pin, creating a foil 1 cm thick. Next, cut it into thin strips and transform them into cords by rolling them in the palm of your hand; pass the pinci through the corn flour and set them aside. Now mince the vegetables and fry them lightly in a pan with a bit of preheated olive oil until they are browned; brown the minced meat and then pour in the Brunello di Montalcino. Turn the flame up to eliminate the residual alcohol and, after about five minutes, lower it again and add hot water to finish cooking the ragout. It will have to cook for a couple of hours to dry out a bit, to ensure that the pinci hold the sauce well. Now cook the pasta in abundant salted water, for about 10-12 minutes, then drain it and pour it into the pan with the ragout; put it back on a moderate flame, and, with the aid of a fork, mix the pasta and sauce. Serve the pinci with grated cheese on the side.

recipe from the CASTELLO DI VELONA restaurant of Castelnuovo dell'Abate (Siena)

first course

Rice with red chicory, Pecorino and Brunello

- 300 g of Vialone Veronese igp midget rice
- 1 average bunch of Chioggia red chicory
- 1 glass of Brunello di Montalcino docg
- 30 g of sheep's milk cheese (Pecorino)
- 1/2 white onion
- 2 dippers of meat broth
- 1 sausage
- 1 spoon of extra virgin olive oil
- 1 spoon of butter
- salt
- red, green and white pepper

Heat the olive oil in a pan over a moderate flame and add the minced onion. Let it welt and throw in the rice. Toast the rice so that it remains slightly hard. After a few minutes add the Chioggia red chicory, of which the leaves will have been separated, washed and cut into pieces; mix everything and pour in the wine. Raise the flame moderately, so as to eliminate the residual alcohol and, when the quantity of wine has been reduced by half, finish cooking the rice, gradually adding dippers of meat broth, which should be boiling to avoid blocking the cooking of the dish. Adjust the taste with a bit of salt. When the rice is finished cooking, but not overcooked, lower the flame as much as possible and whisk it: add a bit of butter and, always mixing, the grated cheese. Remove the skin from the sausage, mince it and add it to the rice, together with the mix of red, white and green pepper, twisted as they are added in. Mix everything together quickly but delicately and serve in single, pre-heated plates.

recipe from the AL GIARDINO osteria of Montalcino (Siena)

second course

Duck with Brunello Grappa

- 1 duck weighing about 1.200 g
- 1/2 glass of Brunello Grappa
- 1 glass of dry white wine
- 2 large white onions
- 4 spoons of extra virgin olive oil
- salt, pepper

Clean the duck and remove the head, gut and remove any eventual remaining feathers from the skin. Flame the duck over the fire to do this, then wash it under a jet of water and dry it off with kitchen paper. Cut the onions into thin slices and set them aside. Grease an oven pan abundantly with extra virgin olive oil, place the salted duck in the pan, pepper it and cover it with the slices of onion. Then place the duck in the oven, which will have been pre-heated to 180° C in the meantime, and let it brown for about thirty minutes. Take it out of the oven and baste it evenly with the Brunello grappa. Place the duck back in the oven for at least another thirty minutes; to prevent the meat from losing tenderness, baste the duck gradually, several times, with spoonfuls of the dry white wine. When it is done, cut the duck into pieces and serve hot, together with the sauce, adding perhaps a bit of raw extra virgin olive oil. This simple dish can be a success if the ingredients are of good quality and the cooking temperature is kept constant.

recipe from the TAVERNA DEI BARBI restaurant of Montalcino (Siena)

second course
Old style 'peposo'

- 1 kg beef cheek
- 1.500 cl of Brunello di Montalcino docg wine
- green pepper and mashed black pepper
- 3 spikes of cloves
- wild fennel flowers (or fennel seeds)
- 2 heads of garlic
- salt, cheesecloth sack

Remove the excess fat from the beef cheek and cut it into nut-sized pieces; salt it and let it macerate with Brunello di Montalcino wine in a tall iron pot. Create a sack of spices with the cheesecloth. Including the green pepper, the mashed black pepper, the clove spikes, the peeled garlic and wild fennel flowers in the cheesecloth sack. Place the sack in the wine to create an infusion. After about three hours (a sufficient length of time to macerate the meat well and make it savoury) place the iron pot with its contents into the oven, which will have been preheated to 160° in the meantime. Let it cook and cover it with a cover with holes to allow the steam to escape; if you haven't got a cover with holes available, use a sheet of aluminium foil, poking holes in it in several points and wrapping it around the border of the pot. Continue cooking the beef cheek for four hours. You will obtain in this manner an extremely soft, savoury and spicy meat, to serve in individual plates with corn meal mush, or 'polenta', which should not be too soft, so that it can be eaten with the cooking sauce.

recipe from the BOCCON DI VINO restaurant of Montalcino (Siena)

second course

Veal titbits with Brunello

- 800 g of veal pulp
- 500 cl of Brunello
  di Montalcino docg
- 1 onion
- 2 carrots
- 1 piece of celery
- sage, rosemary
- 4 cloves of garlic
- 4 spoons of extra virgin
  olive oil
- vegetable broth
- salt

Cut the meat into pieces and place it in an earthenware container with the wine. Leave it to macerate for two hours. In the meantime, mince the vegetables, aromas and cloves of garlic well and place the mixture in an earthenware pot with an abundant dose of extra virgin olive oil, and cook until the mixture welts. Do not let it burn and keep the flame moderate. Mix the lightly fried mixture with a wooden spoon. Remove the meat from the wine, let it drip to drain off the excess wine and add it to the mixture, browning it well. Cook the meat with the wine used for the maceration, adding it to the pot where the tidbits and mixture are cooking. Let it cook slowly for about three hours. If necessary, ad boiling vegetable broth. The meat is done when it falls easily apart when touched with a fork. Serve the veal tidbits with Brunello di Montalcino on individual, pre-heated plates, accompanied by a good Tuscan bread, grilled polenta or a side dish of steamed potatoes.

recipe from the IL POZZO trattoria of Sant'Angelo in Colle (Siena)

second course
Rabbit with Brunello

- 1/2 rabbit
- 2 cloves of garlic
- 1 1/2 hectograms of bacon
- 1 litre of red kitchen wine
- 2 glasses of Brunello di Montalcino docg
- 5 leaves of sage
- extra virgin olive oil, salt

C ut the rabbit half into pieces; let it soak in water for a couple of hours. After this, pour an abundant amount of oil into a pan and add the cloves of garlic, which should be peeled, along with the bacon, cut into small cubes. Without placing over the flame yet, place the rabbit into this cooking base, after letting it drip-drain, and start browning it over a lively flame. When it is golden brown lower the flame, adding the sage and a pinch of salt. Continue cooking, adding dippers of red wine periodically. After about an hour, the wine will be reduced and the rabbit will have almost finished cooking. Make its taste more characteristic by adding the two glasses of Brunello di Montalcino. Turn the flame up and allow the residual alcohol to evaporate, without allowing the cooking base to dry up too much. Serve the rabbit piping hot, accompanied by a couple of abundant spoonfuls of yellow corn meal mush (polenta) and steamed potatoes.

recipe from the GRAPPOLO BLU restaurant of Montalcino (Siena)

second course

Fillet of Chianina covered with Brunello on Zolfini beans

- 2 fillets of 250 gms, one being fillet of Chianina
- 1 bottle of Brunello di Montalcino docg
- 12 slices of pork cheek seasoned cut fine
- 80 gms of Zolfini beans
- 4 garlic cloves
- 2 carrots chopped into little pieces
- 2 stems of celery
- 2 red onions, 3 bay leaves
- 3 sprigs of thyme
- 2 sprigs of rosemary
- 2 sage leaves, parsley
- 10 grains of black pepper
- 3 small balls of juniper
- 1/2 l of dark veal gravy
- cooking salt
- 30 gms of butter
- extra virgin olive oil
- salt, pepper

Leave the beans in water for 12 hours, then put them in a pan with salt and pepper, 1 sprig of rosemary, 1 clove of garlic, sage and 2 spoonfuls of oil. Cook for 4 hours on a low flame and flavour with a little oil. Reduce the wine by half by cooking it on a low flame, adding carrots, celery, onions, pepper grains, juniper, 3 cloves of garlic, bay leaves, thyme, 1 sprig of rosemary and cooking salt, leaving to infuse for 30 minutes. Brown the fillets in a pan on both sides, salt and pepper. Bring the sauce to the boil and add the fillets, covering them and cook for 25 minutes at 80 degrees. Filter the sauce. Add the dark gravy to the sauce and reduce on a lively flame for 3 minute, salt and add the cold butter for binding the sauce. Cut the fillets in half, perpendicular to the fibre. Lay the pork cheek slices in a tin with oven roll and cook at 100 degrees for 90 minutes, until crispy. Serve the fillets on the dish with the beans covered by abundant amounts of sauce and decorate with parsley and slices of crispy pork cheek.

recipe from the BANFI restaurant of Montalcino (Siena)

second course

Breast of Hen-Pheasant with Brunello

- 8 breasts of hen-pheasant
- 50 g of butter
- 40 g of white flour
- 1/2 litre of Brunello di Montalcino docg
- salt

Start preparing the Brunello di Montalcino sauce with which the breast of hen-pheasants will be served. Melt the butter over a pot of boiling water and remove it from the flame for just the amount of time necessary to put the sieved flower into the pan. Put it back on the fire and amalgamate the flour and melted butter, preferably with a wooden spoon. Gradually pour in the Brunello di Montalcino, taking care to mix it continuously with the composition to avoid the formation of lumps. Once the paste has been obtained, bring it to a boil, mixing it continuously for several minutes. Remove it from the flame, add salt and let it rest, keeping it warm. Prepare the breasts of hen-pheasant. Start by removing the skin. In a non-stick pan, heat a bit of oil and cook the hen-pheasant, turning the breasts frequently, so that they are cooked homogenously and the pulp is golden brown. Serve on individual plates, placing two breasts of hen-pheasant on each plate, covered with the Brunello sauce.

recipe from the AL BRUNELLO DI MONTALCINO restaurant of Montalcino (Siena)

museum and folklore

Meeting the protection consortium, Benvenuto Brunello and the folklore events that take place in the territor of Montalcino

9

276 - drum used by one of the figures during the 'feast of the thrush'

277 - Camigliano, the game of the wheel during the feast of the rooster

Museum and folklore

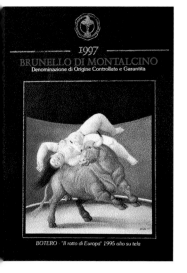

BOTERO - "Il ratto di Europa" 1995 olio su tela

278 - Ferdinando Botero, 'the rat of Europe', 1967, a work provided by the author for the Brunello 'ethical' label

279 - ceremonial plaque of the Brunello di Montalcino vintages of the protection consortium

THE PROMOTIONAL ACTIVITIES OF BRUNELLO

In 1967 the Consortium of Brunello di Montalcino Wine was established, as a free association among the producers, following the recognition of the 'denominazione d'origine controllata' (doc).

The basis for the idea of Brunello is then team work, and its origins, its settings and its future potentiality remaining tied to this synergy between producers, which then forms that solidity of image and proposal that is the guarantee of continuity and prosperity for all.

Subsequently, with these perspectives in mind and a new statute, on the 18th of November 2000 a more modern Consortium came into being, with the 4 consortiums protecting Montalcino wines (Brunello, Rosso, Moscadello and Sant'Antimo) being incorporated into one single body. The adoption of the new regulation of the Consortium was necessary to adapt to the dispositions of law that govern the docg wines and that also precisely define the role and activity of the consortiums. Among the initiatives of greater importance organised by the Consortium there is 'Benvenuto Brunello', which occurs each year at Montalcino in the month of February and which is included in a tour for journalists from the international restaurant and wine trade. Accompanying the tasting moments of the lately harvested vintages, there are titles allocated recognising those who have distinguished themselves in terms of product value: a number of stars is assigned for the deserving vintage, based on the judgement of delegated enologists, who evaluate the structure of the wines and the global quality. Allocated stars are finally celebrated by fixed ceramic plates on the walls of the age old civic hall. From year to year, the realisation of the plate is entrusted to a personality of high esteem from the world of art and culture, who, appreciating Brunello, works to consolidate the idea that wine is also culture. The Consortium has also proposed futures with bottles of Brunello offered by the various companies, that is labels of illustrious names in the international art world, such as Ferdinando Botero, who made himself available for the initiative dedicated to the reconstruction of the bell tower of the church of Sellano, the town that suffered in the Umbrian earthquake.

EVALUATION OF THE QUALITY OF BRUNELLO DI MONTALCINO VINTAGES

Year	Stars	Year	Stars
1945	★★★★★	1974	★★
1946	★★★★	1975	★★★★★
1947	★★★★	1976	★
1948	★★	1977	★★★★
1949	★★★	1978	★★★★
1950	★★★★	1979	★★★★
1951	★★★★	1980	★★★★
1952	★★★	1981	★★★
1953	★★★	1982	★★★★
1954	★★	1983	★★★★
1955	★★★★★	1984	★
1956	★★	1985	★★★★★
1957	★★★★	1986	★★★
1958	★★★★	1987	★★★
1959	★★★	1988	★★★★★
1960	★★★	1989	★★
1961	★★★★★	1990	★★★★★
1962	★★★★	1991	★★★★
1963	★★★	1992	★★★
1964	★★★★★	1993	★★★★
1965	★★★★	1994	★★★★
1966	★★★★	1995	★★★★★
1967	★★★★	1996	★★★
1968	★★★	1997	★★★★★
1969	★★	1998	★★★★
1970	★★★★★	1999	★★★★
1971	★★★	2000	★★★
1972	★	2001	★★★★
1973	★★★	2002	★★

THE STARS OF BRUNELLO

These are the plaques
that have been realised to date,
as a demonstration of the fact
that 'creating art' for Brunello
means testifying to its value

≥80 - Roberto Turchi (1992)

≥81 - Christian Leber (1993)

≥82 - Sandro Chia (1994)

≥83 - Oliviero Toscani (1995)

≥84 - Pierluigi Lolla (1996)

≥85 - Deborah Compagnoni (1997)

≥86 - Ottavio Missoni (1998)

≥87 - Giorgietto Giugiaro (1999)

≥88 - Emilio Giannelli (2000)

≥89 - Miuccia Prada (2001)

≥90 - Roberto Cavalli (2002)

THE MUSEUM OF THE COMMUNITY
OF MONTALCINO AND BRUNELLO

In the restructured stables of the Dei Barbi Farm, the property of the Cinelli Colombini family, museum artefacts have been housed, dedicated to the history and culture of wine. Stefano Cinelli, the owner of the vine tending and producing

291 and 292 - Museum of the community of Montalcino and Brunello, exhibition room

company, has here prepared an exhibition of old agricultural machinery, equipment, working clothes and costumes used for traditional festivals, which stand side by side with a collection of photographic and film documents, available in audio visual rooms set aside for that purpose.

It is a museum which has been conceived with the idea of offering a 'trip' back in time, suggesting paths of anthropological matrixes, not a mute sequence of windows. These objects provide us with a notion of Brunello that is not a product, even if appreciated as such, but also as an added value, symbol of regional identity created by men who have always recognised the character of the lands of the vineyards, handing down their secrets of wine production and utilising technology without forgetting the traditional cellar methods.

THE MUSEUM OF GLASS

The fire, the wine and the glass are the elements that represent the essence of the small museum run by the Fondazione Banfi, which can be visited at the Poggio alle Mura Castle, headquarters of the firm in Montalcino. A whole array of objects of glass working art from the Estruscan and

Roman periods, down to the forms of art of the twentieth century, which are fittingly represented by the works of Salvador Dalì, Jean Cocteau and Pablo Picasso, are exhibited at the museum.

Earth, air, water and fire: these are the four elements. Villa Banfi's tiny museum of glass entirely expresses the identification of the dominance of fire in wine (which contains all of the elements), in relation to its accessory components, that is to say bottles and glasses.

A paste of vitreous materials form amphoras, made precious with decorations, air blown to create translucent bottles and phials, perfection in modern crystal: forms born of fire find hospitality on the shelves of the museum, well guarded in the ancient stables of the castle.

The granite stones and argillaceous badlands reveal fossiliferous deposits, and give birth to bottles that conserve the wine and goblets that contain it for a brief moment.

293 - Montalcino, castle of Poggio alle Mura

294 - 'Porter', Pablo Picasso, museum of glass

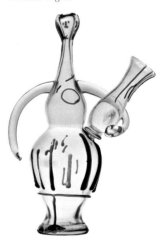

MUSEUM OF GLASS

From ancient times to the modern bottle, a collection that recounts the history of glass, interwoven with the history of wine

295 - english bottle, 17ᵗʰ century

296 - catalan flask, 16ᵗʰ century

297 - greek *oinochòe* , 4ᵗʰ-5ᵗʰ century B.C.

298 - oriental pitcher, 3ʳᵈ-4ᵗʰ century B.C.

299 - english pitchers, 48ᵗʰ century

300 - venetian glass, 18th century

301 - english pitchers, 48th century

302 - 'The Siren', Jean Cocteau, 20th century

303 - french cup, 19th century

304 - english bottle in Naislea style, 18th century

305 - funereal urn, Renania, 1rd-2th century A.D.

THE FEAST OF THE THRUSH

The 'Feast of the Thrush' is held annually in Montalcino. On this occasion, in an austere corner of the fortress and among the suggestive corners of the historical centre, popular feasts are celebrated,

animated by the quarters that historically divide the city, representations that people still participate in today with a deep sense of belonging.

The archery tournament at the Feast of the Thrush has expert archers from the different quarters committed in the competition between the Borghetto, the Pianello, the Ruga and the Travaglio, the four 'cloves' into which Montalcino is divided. The historical parade is carried out with hundreds of figures dressed in medieval costumes, who present quality agricultural products and the foods prepared by able homemakers of the quarter. Such are the most genuine components of these traditional feasts.

In thirty minutes, the archers (who must be Ilcinese doc, according to the regulations), must demonstrate their de-

306 and 307 - the feast of the thrush

termination by conquering the silver arrow, which will mark the supremacy of the quarter where the archer lives throughout the year.

The contest is instinctive and the target is in the shape of a wild boar, an animal that is a symbol of these woods and which was sacred even for the Etruscans, who were al-

so great hunters. The targets are exposed for a few seconds, just enough time to allow each archer to slot his arrows and take five shots at the moving animal-shapes.

308 - target practice

The distances from the targets are comparable to what can be determined in an actual hunt for wild boar, ranging from 25 to 45 meters from the targets. A 'citizen captain' dominates the playing field. In addition to assigning the victory, he operates an hourglass that marks the time taken to shoot the arrows. He also operates the lever that moves the boar-shaped targets along their respective runways for the shooting contest at each distance, which the two archers for every quarter, chosen by casting lots on the first day, must perform.

309 - archery

The archery tournament is not a sports competition. At this feast, the population of Montalcino celebrates the medieval customs of the time when hunting was done in the rich and vast woods of the city. And, at the end of every hunt in those far away times, the feast was great and everyone enjoyed it. This also happens in our own day, as the banquet satisfies the mastery of the quarters competing with each other and the commitment of the women in preparing good food for all of the participants.

FIGURES AT THE FEAST OF THE THRUSH

Montalcino returns
to the magical Middle Ages:
the people dress in the fashion
of the time and vie to win
the silver arrow

THE OTHER FEASTS

Another popular feast celebrated in the territory of Montalcino is the 'Feast of the Rooster'. It takes place in Camigliano, at the beginning of the autumn season, and is realised by cooking hundreds of farm chickens over hot coals on a spit, doused with litres of local wine. This too, is a long-awaited feast every year, where visitors from all over Tuscany participate.

 321 - thrush

322 - the feast of the rooster

The tournament opening the hunting season is scheduled for the second Sunday in August and marks the beginning of erstwhile hunting parties, while the Feast of the Thrush, which is scheduled for the last Sunday in October, allows the inhabitants to relive the culmination of the hunting season.

On the day of the hunting tournament the lovely streets and beautiful squares of the town are full of musical trumpeters and excited drummers, there to announce the grand opening moment of this year's hunting season, while in the

afternoon a parade of cavaliers and dames, who take a walk to the fortress, where the archers form the four quarters of Borghetto, Pianello, Ruga and Travaglio vie for victory, challenging each other in an archery contest.

The archers, two for each quarter, are chosen by casting lots among three of the proposed participants of the competition. They must strike, with bows that do not have aiming sights, the four silhouettes of boar placed on tracks, which are also assigned by casting lots. Each archer shoots 5 arrows every time, through four sets, where distance is gradually increased, and then the score is counted up; naturally, the quarter that has the largest number of points wins.

the producers

After our account of the history of this wine, we present some of the producers of Brunello di Montalcino. The following is a description of 28 vineyards, where the products spoken of in this volume can be found

10

ALTESINO

ALTESINO spa
✉ località Altesino - 53024 Montalcino (Siena)
☎ +39 0577 806208
🖨 +39 0577 806131
✉ altesino@iol.it

THE WINES

Brunello di Montalcino docg,
Brunello di Montalcino docg
'Montosoli',
Rosso di Montalcino doc,
Bianco di Altesino,
Rosso di Altesino,
Alte d'Altesi,
Palazzo Altesi,
Vin Santo d'Altesi doc

Among the eastern hills of Montalcino rises the austere mass of the thirteenth century Altesi palace, built by the Tuscan family of the same name, whose coat of arms is still visible, set above the original oaken portal.

Around the building 65 the 64 hectares of the Altesino vineyard are spread, of which 27 are a specialised vineyard, divided into thre cru of Brunello (Altesino, La Velona and Montosoli).

Claudio Basla, winemaker and curator of the interests of the Altesino company, which is the property of Elisabetta Gnudi Angelini, works in close contact, shoulder to shoulder with the enologist Pietro Rivella.

The vineyard is a precursor of the various and important structural innovations that have involved Brunello di Montalcino for the past thirty years. As early as 1979, the French barrique was being introduced in this territory, thanks to Altesino. The propulsive thrust of this company is also revealed in the introduction of the concept of the cru: Montosoli, long noted for the production of extremely elegant wines, was in fact the first cru in the Ilcinese territory. It must also be said that the first futures, that is to say the advance sale of Brunello to be marketed five years later, were printed by this firm in 1985. Finally, the crowning glory of the research performed in the rationalisation of the vineyard's productive process, even the first Brunello grappa saw the light among the historical cellars of Altesi palace.

The Altesino, tanks to their Montosoli cru, obtained an important international recognition when the Wine Spectator, the most prestigious enological magazine in the anglo-saxon panorama, defined it as the second most representative Italian vineyard.

OTHER PRODUCTS

Brunello Altesino brandy, Brunello Altesino grappa, Brunello Altesino Reserve grappa, extra virgin olive oil

ARGIANO

ARGIANO srl
- Sant'Angelo in colle - 53024 Montalcino (Siena)
- ☎ +39 0577 844037
- 📠 +39 0577 844210
- ✉ argiano@argiano.net
- 🖥 www.argiano.net

THE WINES
Brunello di Montalcino docg,
Rosso di Montalcino doc,
Solengo igt, Suolo igt

Villa Argiano, with its Medicean dimensions, dominates the vined high plain that spreads southwards from the hilly Ilcinese land. This is the headquarters of the wine tending and producing company of the Argiano Estate. Founded in 1580, it has passed in recent times to the countess Noemi Marone Cinzano.

Among the beauties of the site, other than the surrounding environment made up of vineyards and woods, there is the splendid cellar, located under the villa itself, where the wine ages in French oak drums of small and medium-size with temperature and humidity at a constant level and without light or sound.

Since 1992 the company has been travelling on a dynamic journey directed towards vine tending and production of high quality with the countess as guide, availing herself of the enologist Giacomo Tachis' advice. This all means that the company has achieved recognition in both national and international markets. Their Brunello di Montalcino and Rosso, cared for and promoted by the business manager Pepe Schib Graciani and by technical manager Giampiero Pazzaglia, are today placed side by side with two wines of the 'Super Tuscan' category, Solengo and il Suolo. The wines produced on the Argiano estate are appreciated by conniosseurs and by enology critics alike, specialised in terms of their type, their unity, with a decidedly international taste.

Being noted also for the care afforded to the organolectic traditions of the land, the company has arranged for the revival of bottles of different great reserves from its heritage, bringing the operation of 'historic vintages of Brunello di Montalcino' to life.

There are six selected products: 1973, 1975, 1977, 1978, 1979 and 1980.

OTHER PRODUCTS
extra virgin olive oil

BANFI

BANFI srl
Castello di Poggio alle Mura - 53024 Montalcino (Siena)
☎ +39 0577 840111
🖹 +39 0577 840471
✉ banfi@banfi.it
🖥 www.castellobanfi.com

THE WINES

Brunello di Montalcino docg,
Brunello di Montalcino docg
'Poggio alle Mura',
Brunello di Montalcino docg
'Poggio all'Oro',
Moscadello di Montalcino doc,
Rosso di Montalcino doc,
Sant'Antimo doc 'Colvecchio',
Sant'Antimo doc 'Cum Laude',
Sant'Antimo doc 'Excelsus',
Sant'Antimo doc 'Fontanelle',
Sant'Antimo doc 'Mandrielle',
Sant'Antimo doc 'Sant'Angelo'
Sant'Antimo doc 'Serena',
Sant'Antimo doc 'Summus',
Sant'Antimo doc 'Tavernelle'

It's not easy to describe in a brief profile everything the proprietors and creators of this company, the Italian American Mariani family, have done for the growth and valorisation of the territory of Montalcino through the promotion of cultural activities and the diffusion of their wines. Starting from the re-launching of the local historical product par excellence, Moscadello, right down to the creation of Brunello, Banfi is definitely a great protagonist, at the cutting edge of a vast and extremely personalised international wine production.

Banfi's headquarters is in the Poggio alle Mura Castle, whose enormous bulk stands out against the Grosseto maremma plains. The company represents the closing of the circle of a peculiar economic system found only in the area surrounding Montalcino: a system that unites local arts and traditions with industrial development, maintaining great respect for nature, a value often absent in other similar organisations operating in other divisions.

The city of Montalcino owes a lot to the John Mariani family, who have succeeded in valorising the local and external human resources employed, rewarding the career of many important 'men of wine', promoting the qualification of the territories excluded from the Brunello roll, by supporting Sant'Antimo doc and launching the name of Tuscany docg red on markets all over the world.

Banfi's Brunello docg and *cru* Poggio all'Oro are produced on 170 hectares of Sangiovese vines, in the south at 250 m. The vinification, derived from grapes selected before they even leave the vineyard, takes place in extremely modern wine cellars, with refinement in choice durmast oak casks built by the vineyard itself.

OTHER PRODUCTS

Plum acquavita spirit,
Moscadello acquavita spirit,
Brunello grappa,
Moscadello grappa,
extra virgin olive oil,
honey, plum jam,
pre-packed plums,
Etruscan balsamic sauce

BIONDI SANTI

TENUTA GREPPO
di Franco Biondi Santi
località Greppo, 183 - 53024 Montalcino (Siena)
☎ +39 0577 848087
📠 +39 0577 849396
✉ biondisanti@biondisanti.it
🖥 www.biondisanti.it

THE WINES
Brunello di Montalcino
docg 'Annata',
Brunello di Montalcino
docg Riserva,
Rosso di Montalcino doc

It was Ferruccio Biondi Santi who started the rational management of the Greppo estate; his decision played an extremely important role in grafting new vines of a firm with a Sangiovese grosso clone, which he selected himself.

Today the estate has an area, cultivated in vineyards, of 19 hectares, all of which is Brunello. In the choice of terrains, it is normal to discard the most fertile ones, and to prefer terrain with argillaceous shale. The counter-espalier system of vinegrowing is used, with horizontal barbed cord.

In the Franco Biondi Santi vineyards, the two most important operations in cultivating the vines is the thinning of grapes and the manual selection of the grapes at harvest time, which permits directing only first choice grapes towards the production of Brunello di Montalcino. The Greppo cellar has not undergone a great many modernisations, except for the introduction of modern and adequately equipped technological installations.

The grapes, after pressing, ferment in the great cement vats and tubs for up to 15 or 20 days, at controlled temperature. During tumultuous fermentation, two remixing operations are performed every day, and the marc cap is kept humid with manual intervention. After the wine is drawn off, malolactic fermentation is favoured, maintaining the environment at a temperature of 18° for a period of 30 days.

In the April after the harvest the new wine is placed in durmast oak casks from Slavonia for refinement. At the end of the fourth year, it is finally bottled in 0.75 litre Bordeaux bottles.

Biondi Santi Brunello is not marketed before six months after bottling and is exported world wide.

OTHER PRODUCTS

extra virgin olive oil

BOLSIGNANO

AZIENDA AGRICOLA BOLSIGNANO
di fratelli Rubegni ss
podere Bolsignano, 272- 53024 Montalcino (Siena)
☎ +39 0577 848577
📠 +39 0577 848577
✉ bolsignano@tin.it

THE WINES
Brunello di Montalcino docg,
Rosso di Montalcino doc,
'Il Chiostro'

Roberto Rebegni is the young master of the Bolsignano vineyard, who takes care of the building complex of ancient origins, surrounded by 7.5 hectares of vineyards, of which three are dedicated to Sangiovese which could become Brunello di Montalcino. He is assisted in his work by his younger sisters Elisabetta and Giulia. Bolsignano is therefore a family-run business, where ancient traditions, like the strong community spirit displayed by the parents, childrens and acquired relatives, who are comfortable with the lifestyle of past times.

The territory where the main body of the company is located is in a high area that faces the extended terrace of the plains that flow down towards the Ombrone River. The vineyard is therefore located on the western side of the Ilcinese 'pyramid', which enjoys warmer marine breezes and higher temperatures, both in summer and winter. It is a dryish land, with clay shale and tuffaceous terrain, which often stresses the vines, conferring that quality of slow opening up of aromas upon uncorking the bottle, that only great refined wines possess.

The full and powerful body is therefore the primary characteristic of the wines produced at Bolsignano.

The production of Brunello di Montalcino is currently less than 5,000 bottles annually, a number that is in any case destined to grow when new plants begin producing. The aging is done rigorously in 30 hectolitre durmast oak casks, as required by the tradition of the most genuine Brunello.

The young age of these winegrowers, together with their passion for their work, places this company among the emerging new realities, destined to become the spokesmen of the enological tradition of this land.

OTHER PRODUCTS
Brunello grappa

CASISANO COLOMBAIO

FATTORIA CASISANO COLOMBAIO
di Tatiana Schwarze
località Casisano - 53024 Montalcino (Siena)
☎ +39 0577 835540 and +39 335 5248636
📠 +39 0577 835540
✉ info@brunello.org
🖥 www.brunello.org

THE WINES

Brunello di Montalcino docg,
Brunello di Montalcino
docg Riserva,
Brunello di Montalcino docg
'Vigna del Colombaiolo',
Moscadello di Montalcino doc,
Rosso di Montalcino doc,
Rosso di Montalcino doc
'Colombaiolo',
Casisano Rosso igt

In splendid isolation among the quiet Tuscan hills, completely surrounded by vineyards and centuries-old woods, the Casisano Colombaio Farm stands out, where wines come from using grapes grown in 2 different zones, far from each other but both excellently located in pedoclimatic terms. The total spread of the company reaches 60 hectares, 19 of which are vineyard and 9 olive grove. The double name of the farm in fact derives from the same names of the two vined zones that form the supporting structure. The Colombaio holding is solidly planted on the inaccessible slopes, situated halfway down the hill of Montalcino.

The Casisano is a natural terrace which dominates the area south-east of the Montalcino territory, between the abbey of Sant'Antimo and the valley of the Orcia river.

In the quiet of its cellars the precious wines of the farm age.

In fact, we have here an evocative looking cellar with monumental and modern architectonic shapes that welcome visitors to the sight of Slavonic oak casks and French oak barriques, while the bottles of Brunello di Montalcino of various vintages are to be savoured in the very special tasting room, above the cellar, as you gaze from windows and admire the wild surrounding landscape. Riccardo Ciarpella, son of the proprietor, Tatiana Schwarze, is the person who has the task of managing the company in its various phases, following with special caring attention the Sangiovese Grosso vines, from where Brunello di Montalcino comes, vintage and cru, this latter obtained only using the grapes of the same vineyard, Colombaiolo.

Rosso di Montalcino comes from that vineyard too, being elaborated in a different way .

OTHER PRODUCTS
Brunello grappa,
Brunello Reserve grappa,
extra virgin olive oil

CASTELLO DI CAMIGLIANO

CASTELLO DI CAMIGLIANO srl
via d'Ingresso, 2 - località Camigliano - 53024 Montalcino (Siena)
☎ +39 0577 844068 and 0577 816061
🖨 +39 0577 816040
✉ info@camigliano.it and camigliano@virgilio.it
🖥 www.camigliano.it

THE WINES

Brunello di Montalcino docg,
Brunello di Montalcino docg
'Gualto' Selezione,
Rosso di Montalcino doc,
Sant'Antimo doc Cabernet
Sauvignon,
Poderuccio igt

A lovely township greets the visitor as soon as he passes the sign that indicates the beginning of Camigliano and the end of the only road that will bring him there.

Camigliano castle is still inhabited today by about thirty residents, some of whom are occupied in the work of the wine producing concerns and the surrounding fields, distributed over 530 hectares all around the houses. The company has a total of 91 vined hectares, from which 50 are destined for the production of Brunello di Montalcino base and its 'Gualto' selection, produced for the first time with the 1998 vintage.

The Brunello that Gualtiero and Laura Ghezzi produce at Camigliano is a particularly, warm and elegant elaboration, that comes from the grapes from the vines exposed to the south of Montalcino, along the sweet slopes that descend towards the Maremma, on land rich in tuff and argillaceous soil.

The art of making wine is reflected then in the images that glimpses of the age-old township evoke in the visitor, above all the evocative historic cellar of the castle, for long decades consecrated only by the ageing of Brunello di Montalcino and today the offering of hospitality for shows and tasting.

Next to the old cellar, where the Brunello and the other company wines are effectively produced and preserved, there is the very new underground cellar, provided with all the most up-to-date technology, while avoiding any kind of environmental impact. The distribution of the working phases has been studied in such a way as to allow an elaboration of the wine 'a cascata' (cascaded), reducing to a minimum the use of pumps for further preserving the organolectic characteristics of the Camigliano wines.

OTHER PRODUCTS

Brunello grappa,
extra virgin olive oil dop
'Terre di Siena'

CASTELLO ROMITORIO

AZIENDA AGRICOLA
CASTELLO ROMITORIO srl
☑ località Romitorio, 279 - 53024 Montalcino (Siena)
☎ +39 0577 897220
🖹 +39 0577 897026
✉ info@castelloromitorio.it
🖳 www.castelloromitorio.com

THE WINES
Brunello di Montalcino docg,
Brunello di Montalcino
docg Riserva,
Rosso di Montalcino doc,
Sant'Antimo doc 'Romito
del Romitorio',
Sant'Antimo Bianco doc
Chardonnay,
Brio Toscano igt,
Chianti Colli Senesi docg

A legend tells of Romitorio Castle, a massive and suggestive XII century fortress positioned in the Montalcino hills, which is said to have been built in a single night with the magical assistance of a saint.

As further testimony of the influence this place has always had on the local population, it is also said that there is a spacious escape tunnel that passes underground in wide ditches and through leafy forests, to connect the Montalcino fortress to the Castle basement.

Today the Romitorio is simply the dwelling and company headquarters of Sandro Chia, the internationally famous artist, whose passion and artistic vision restored the abandoned castle to life and valorised its cellar.

The first wine was bottled in 1987. In addition to building a cellar whose structure is a testimony of his artistic expression, Sandro Chia, assisted by his friend Carlo Vittori, approached wine as if it were an extension of his art: the illustrious exponent of Italian trans-vanguard art loves to assert that he *"creates his wine like he creates a painting"*.

Sandro Chia adds another treat to his scrupulous cultivation and wine-making: a collection of labels that describe the products through his important works of art, so that the Bordeaux-style bottle, which contains Brunello di Montalcino, becomes an object of cult and a collectors' item.

He also recently launched a cru, Brunello di Montalcino 1997, which he intends to offer as the best of the company's production, with vinification only from grapes of the most important vineyards. A white wine and four other types of reds complete the range of wines produced.

OTHER PRODUCTS

Brunello vintage Grappa, Brunello Grappa aged, extra virgin olive oil

CIACCI PICCOLOMINI D'ARAGONA

CIACCI PICCOLOMINI D'ARAGONA
Borgo di Mezzo, 62 - 53020 Castelnuovo dell'Abate (Siena)
☎ +39 0577 835616
▤ +39 0577 835785
✉ info@ciaccipiccolomini.com
🖥 www.ciaccipiccolomini.com

THE WINES
Brunello di Montalcino docg,
Rosso di Montalcino doc,
Sant'Antimo doc 'Ateo',
Sant'Antimo doc 'Fabius',
Montecucco doc

The estate of Ciacci Piccolomini d'Aragona guards its historical patrimony in a splendid palace, built in 1672 by Fabius De Vecchis, who was then Bishop of Montalcino. Today, in the historical cellars, several vintages of Brunello di Montalcino are maturing in durmast oak casks from Slavonia, of various sizes.

Ciacci Piccolomini d'Aragona is a name that has left its mark in history: this family which gave birth to Enea Silvio Piccolomini, better known as Pope Pius II, has left a tangible sign of its importance throughout the Sienese territory.

In 1985, when the noble house was extinguished, the property was inherited by Giuseppe Bianchini and his family, who have gathered the vast historical patrimony, committing themselves to the further qualification of the farm. Since then, they have carried forward the traditions handed down to them with determination.

The company, directed with passion by Giuseppe Bianchini, with the assistance of his children Paolo and Lucia, includes an extension of 200 hectares, of which 35 are given over to vineyards and 40 are planted in olive groves, while the remaining 125 are divided between semi-wild, woods and pasture.

The current production of wine is around 1,400 hectolitres. Bianchini's Brunello is an austere wine, which possesses a fine chromatic presentation, full perfumes, important structure and quite prolonged persistence.

Alongside the organoleptic characteristics of the product, there exists a value of protection of the denomination itself: the microchips recently applied to bottle labels impede falsifiction and guarantee the consumer complete traceability of the docg.

OTHER PRODUCTS

Brunello grappa,
extra virgin olive oil,
honey

COL D'ORCIA

TENUTA COL D'ORCIA spa
✉ località Sant'Angelo in Colle - 53024 Montalcino (Siena)
☎ +39 0577 80891
🖷 +39 0577 808063
✉ coldorcia.direzione@tin.it
🖥 www.coldorcia.it

COL D'ORCIA

THE WINES

Brunello di Montalcino docg,
Brunello di Montalcino docg
Riserva 'Poggio al Vento',
Moscadello di Montalcino
doc 'Pascena',
Rosso di Montalcino doc,
Rosso di Montalcino
doc 'Banditella',
Sant'Antimo Pinot grigio doc,
Cabernet di Toscana igt
'Olmaia',
Chianti docg 'Gineprone',
Toscana igt 'Ghiaie Bianche',
Toscana igt 'Nearco',
Toscana igt 'Rosso
degli Spezieri'

The Col d'Orcia Estate is to be found on the southern side of the community of Montalcino, approximately at 450 metres above sea level, with a climate which shows the influence of its proximity to the Mediterranean, as the crow flies only 35 kilometres away.

The origins of the holding go back to the first half of the 17th century, when the family of the noble cavaliers Della Ciaia established a vast property near to Sant'Angelo. In 1973 the count Alberto Marone Cinzano acquired the company with the aim of contributing to the development and the consolidation of Montalcino on the world markets. Since 1992 the Col d'Orcia Estate has been held in ownership by the son, Francesco Marone Cinzano.

The attention and efforts of the company are constantly concentrated on the development of the potentiality of the land, with wines produced exclusively with grapes cultivated by the company, strongly characterised by type, provided with strong personality and able to distinguish themselves both in terms of wine producing of traditional grapes, such as Sangiovese, as well as for the use of international varieties like Cabernet, Merlot and Syrah.

The vineyards are very well looked after, with thinning of bunches at ripening and erosion management, to reduce the vegetative vigour of the vines, obtaining a lower yield per plant in a natural way.

Starting from the 1997 harvest, with the entry into production of the first vineyards derived from clone selection, the quality and personality of Brunello has been augmented in a progressive manner.

Harvesting is done by hand, with selection of best bunches and ageing of wine is in Slavonic oak casks and Allier and in barriques of French oak.

OTHER PRODUCTS

Brunello grappa,
'Poggio al vento'
Brunello grappa,
Moscadello di Montalcino
'Pascena' grappa,
Cabernet 'Olmaia' grappa,
extra virgin olive oil

CORTE PAVONE

CORTE
PAVONE

LOACKER · CORTE PAVONE
✉ località Corte Pavone - 53024 Montalcino (Siena)
☎ +39 0577 848110 and +39 0471 365125
🖨 +39 0577 846442 and +39 0471 365313
✉ lo@cker.it
🖥 www.loacker. net

THE WINES
Brunello di Montalcino docg,
Rosso di Montalcino doc

Rainer Loacker and his sons began producing Brunello di Montalcino in 1996, continuing in the long wake of brilliant successes in the field of wine making in their land of origin, the Upper Adige River Valley.

The first year of Brunello production coincides with the arrival of the Loakers in this area of Etruria, where they created a vineyard of considerable dimensions. There are a total of about 90 hectares, located at an altitude between 420 and 500 m, of which 12 are cultivated with Sangiovese vines, with a presence of an additional 4 hectares dedicated to other international vines.

From the outset of this adventure, Rainer Loaker and his sons did not hide their ambition to become a point of reference for quality in the Ilcinese territory, in as short a time as possible.

Between the shale and clay buttresses north of the capital, which overlook the distant city of Siena, the Loaker family manages vineyards that all have south-southeast exposure, according to the dictates of biological cultivation, specialising in the most extreme discipline of organic and biodynamic agriculture.

Corte Pavone has banished genetic manipulation and any intervention is aimed at helping the original character to emerge, the very spirit of the precious grapes.

Thus, a fresh, dry Brunello with a good level of acidity and great structure is born. The influence of new woods appears to be important, as they confer international elegance upon the wine. The cellar, built by Loaker on the summit of the Corte Pavone hill, is an architectural structure with great volumes, suitable to host conventions, seminars and wine tasting sessions, in addition to conserving the precious bottles of Brunello.

COSTANTI

AZIENDA AGRARIA CONTI COSTANTI
✉ Colle al Matrichese - 53024 Montalcino (Siena)
☎ +39 0577 848195
🖷 +39 0577 849349
✉ costanti@inwind.it

THE WINES

Brunello di Montalcino docg,
Brunello di Montalcino
docg Riserva,
Rosso di Montalcino doc,

The fifteenth century villa known as 'Colle al Matrichese' has been the residence of the Costanti family since the mid-sixteenth century; in this area there are vineyards that have been cultivated since the eighth century. It was from these vineyards that Tito Costanti, in 1870, produced the two bottles, both of which were called 'Brunello', which were presented at one of the first exhibitions of quality wine from the Sienese lands, dated respectively 1865 and 1869, the first official representatives of the birth of the Ilcinese wine. It is surprising how, in these two enological creations, the structure of what modern regulations dictate for the production of Brunello docg and Rosso di Montalcino doc was already marked out.

In fact, on that occasion the first wine aged five years was presented and was called Brunello, as well as another wine with the same name, although it was aged only one year.

In later years it was Emilio Costanti who dedicated himself to realising the fruits of the research of his predecessor, Tito, making the vineyard at Colle al Matrichese productive. The firm has been managed since 1983 by Adrea Costanti, who avails himself of the consultancy of Vittorio Fiore.

The Brunello produced at this vineyard tends to conserve a great degree of elegance, exalting a refined quality and acidity, the product of a careful interpretation of the territory, in order to give an exclusive personality to the wine.

The company, which borders with the centre of Montalcino, has an extension of about 25 hectares, of which 10 are cultivated with Brunello vines, characterised by a poor terrain in organic substances, with a prevalence of clay shale of the cretaceous age.

DONATELLA CINELLI COLOMBINI

AZIENDA AGRICOLA DONATELLA CINELLI COLOMBINI
'Casato Prime Donne'
- località Casato - 53024 Montalcino (Siena)
- ☎ +39 0577 662108 and +39 0577 849421
- 🖨 +39 0577 662202 and +39 0577 849363
- ✉ holiday@cinellicolombini.it and vino@cinellicolombini.it
- 🖳 www.cinellicolombini.it

Located on the first foothills that climb up towards Montalcino, with a view of Siena's far-off towers, the Casato Prime Donne Farm has belonged to the Donatella Cinelli Colombini family since the now distant 1592. The family's ancestors cultivated the area at that time, utilising the land for hunting and short vacations. It is not by chance that this vineyard has a pronounced womanly nature: over the last four generations, the property has been transmitted exclusively through feminine lines. Today it is Donatella, one of the most noted and highly appraised Ladies of Wine, who holds the reigns of the company's destiny, but daughter Violante is already receiving her mother's first loving, expert indications for a future that has cast her in the role of heir to the family's vineyard patrimony.

The organisational activity of the volcanic Donatella Cinelli Colombini have revolutionised the world of Ital-

THE WINES

Brunello di Montalcino docg,
Brunello di Montalcino docg
'Progetto Prime Donne',
Rosso di Montalcino doc,
Cenerentola doc 'Orcia',
Chianti Superiore docg,
Leone rosso Toscana igt,
Vin Santo doc
'Colli dell'Etruria Centrale'

ian wine, and not only Italian wine, over the last fifteen years. Donatella has inspired, built and guided the Movement of Wine Tourism for a decade, supplying all of the best Italian vineyards with promotional instruments for the substantial growth of quality that has enabled Italian wine to triumph on the international level today.

For some time now, when the diary allows, she has spent her time almost wholly on the Prime Donne project, seeing the birth of a 'female' cellar , where the ingenious producer, with a special line of Brunello wines, intends to demonstrate that *"great enology does not depend on muscles or sex, but only on intelligence"*. The 'Prime Donne' Brunello Project is entirely selected by women tasters of an international calibre, while the vintage Brunello is born in two vineyards of 19 hectares, on the boundaries of the company headquarters.

OTHER PRODUCTS

Brunello grappa,
Chianti Grappa,
extra virgin olive oil

FANTI
TENUTA SAN FILIPPO

FANTI
TENUTA SAN FILIPPO

FANTI - TENUTA SAN FILIPPO
di Baldassarre Filippo Fanti
🖃 via Borgo di Mezzo, 15 - 53020 Castelnuovo dell'Abate (Siena)
☎ +39 0577 835628
🖹 +39 0577 835523
✉ balfant@tin.it

THE WINES
Brunello di Montalcino docg,
Rosso di Montalcino doc,
Sant'Antimo Bianco doc,
Sant'Antimo Rosso doc,
Svoltone, Vin Santo

Baldassarre Filippo Fanti, the current president of the Brunello di Montalcino Consortium, received one of his two names from the founder of the company, who created the vineyard in the initial years of the nineteenth century.

The vineyards were already spread over the company property at that early date, on the tops of the hillsides that surround the village of Castelnuovo dell'Abate, adjacent to the magnificent Abbacy of Sant'Antimo.

The current modern asset of the vineyards was established, in any case, by Filippo Fanti, who enlarged it to today's 40 hectares. The agronomic philosophy behind these goals is oriented towards maintaining an innovative solution: the area between vines is kept narrow, with a high density of plants.

Baldassarre Filippo Fanti's intervention, in any case, is not limited to plan-ting new vines, but takes concrete form in the improvement of techniques of vinificationand refinement in barrels of small dimensions, the containers which have today almost replaced the great traditional barrels.

The wine of the Fanti cellar is destined to remain sincere and accessible in terms of price, to the extent that the producer does not feel it necessary to devote even a small part of it to Reserve. *"Vintage Brunello represents the heart of the vineyard and must express, for better or worse, all of the characteristics of the period that it was produced in"*, asserts Fanti, to confirm this aversion of his for the local wine aged for longer periods of time.

The future of the firm will definitely be entrusted to feminine hands: Fanti's daughters Elisa, who is oriented towards an agronomical education, and Elena, who is interested in international public relations, will one day stand at the helm of the firm.

OTHER PRODUCTS

Rosso Grappa,
Brunello grappa,
extra virgin olive oil

FATTORIA DEI BARBI

FATTORIA DEI BARBI
località Pordenovi, 170 - 53024 Montalcino (Siena)
+39 0577 841111
+39 0577 841112
info@fattoriadeibarbi.it
www.fattoriadeibarbi.it

THE WINES

Brunello di Montalcino docg,
Brunello di Montalcino
docg Riserva,
Brunello di Montalcino docg
'Vigna del Fiore',
Rosso di Montalcino doc,
Chianti delle Colline
Senesi docg,
Morellino di Scansano doc,
Birbone dei Barbi igt 'Toscana',
Brusco dei Barbi igt 'Toscana',
Rosso dei Barbi igt 'Toscana',
Vin Santo doc
'Colli dell'Etruria Centrale'

Woman of Wine *'ante litteram'*, Francesca Cinelli Colombini has given a free hand to her children, and Stefano has taken over the management of one of the vineyard jewels of the family, the Barbi farm.

Located to the east of Monalcino, the farm has an extension of vineyards over an area of 86 hectares, with a productive capacity of 250 thousand bottles of vintage Brunello.

A few thousand bottles of Reserve are produced in the most favourable years. The company overview is wound up with a Brunello cru, 'Vigna del Fiore', created from grapes grown on 5.7 hectares, locted in an area where the vine has been acclimatised for more than 500 years.

Although he comes from such a glorious enological past, Stefano Cinelli Colombini has made modernity a supporting concept in his enterprise. The genuine expression of the territory, as the current trends suggest, have always been the main characteristics of the Barbi farm, filtered through research and experimentation in cloning Sangiovese, and enlarged to its evolution only on land with a vocation: zoning.

A jealous cultivator of his family history, through an innate cultural disposition, Stefano Cinelli Colombini has made this shared history one of the instruments of valorisation for the entire Ilcinese community, building up important places in the common memory and making them available to everyone who wishes to recall the events that led to today's panorama.

The imposing historical cellar, where great Slavonian barrels still find refuge in the bowels of the earth, represents a worthy cross section of the life of the first and most glorious vineyards in Montalcino.

OTHER PRODUCTS

Dei Barbi Grappa, Brunello Grappa, Grappa Reserve, extra virgin olive oil, salted cold ham, Tuscan salami, salamino al Brunello, fresh dried sausages, finocchiona, rustic pâté dei Barbi, dry cheese, semi-dried and fresh, raviggiolo, ricotta cheese

GORELLI
LE POTAZZINE

LE POTAZZINE
località Le Prata - 53024 Montalcino (Siena)
☎ +39 0577 846168
🖹 +39 0577 847974 and +39 0577 849418
✉ tenuta@lepotazzine.it

THE WINES
Brunello di Montalcino docg,
Rosso di Montalcino doc

The name in dialect attributed to the company when it was founded in 1993, 'Potazzine', was taken from the affectionate name with which Giuseppe Gorelli's mother-in-law called her granddaughters; 'potazzine', in fact, are titmice, the lively little birds that inhabit the Tuscan countryside. The farm, which has grown in size over the years, recently saw the completion of a modern new cellar, with separate sections for winemaking and aging.

When working at full capacity, the winery run by Giuseppe Gorelli, enologist and author of wine, produces about fifteen thousand bottles of Brunello per year, with the simple concept that wine should always be pleasing to drink. Drinking pleasure is due to the soft, elegant tannins obtained through careful vinification, with extremely long grape macerations and 'free' fermentation, that is to say a type of fermentation that is not 'managed' through the addition of yeasts, and which leaves the task of bringing the desired results to the wine to the natural components that are already present in the grapes.

The Potazzine Brunello, currently oriented towards large casks, is assembled from two vineyards located in different areas of Montalcino. The vivacity and freshness of grapes cultivated in the Le Prata area, to the west, are united with the substance and body of grapes from the La Torre area, which is located further south. Today the company is in the process of enlarging their installations for Sangiovese grosso. Giuseppe Gorelli does enology consultancy for other local growers, The passion his family nurtures for Brunello is shown by his wife Gigliola. She runs a beautiful and well-supplied bottle-making industry, called 'Montalcino Produce', in the historical centre of the town.

OTHER PRODUCTS
Brunello grappa

LAMBARDI

AZIENDA AGRICOLA CANALICCHIO DI SOTTO
di Maurizio Lambardi
✉ podere Canalicchio di Sotto, 8 - 53024 Montalcino (Siena)
☎ +39 0577 848476
📠 +39 0577 846507
✉ canalicchiodisotto@virgilio.it

LAMBARDI

THE WINES
Brunello di Montalcino docg,
Rosso di Montalcino doc,
Sant'Antimo Bianco doc

Canalicchio di sotto is the name connected to the portion of hill-side vineyard that surrounds the city of Montalcino towards the Val d'Arbia.

Already famous in the nineteenth century and described in Leopol-dine cadastral documents as a 'vined' parcel, Canalicchio di sotto is today run by the Lambardi family.

Maurizio, today's head of the fami-ly, has rationalised his winegrowing firm, conferring it with criteria of functional efficiency and business dynamism in pace with the times.

In restructuring the estate, the cel-lar and renewing the machinery, ac-tion was taken without losing the close contact with the land and na-ture, represented in this case by the small but glorious vineyard, which extends over an area of 6 of the com-pany's 22 hectares.

Located on the sunny side of the hill, at an altitude of 320 metres, the three Brunello vineyards, respectively called 'the old vineyard', the 'new vineyard' and the 'Poggio Vineyard', the plantations have rows that trace the traditional planting methods, three metres each, and produce grapes obtained from a particular clone of Sangiovese grosso, raised with the double barbed cord system.

In the vinifiction celler there is room for 850 hectolitres of tubs and 370 hectolitres in wooden barrels, where the operation of passing from the fragrance of mature grapes to drawing off the wine is performed with careful precision. There will be no small barriques for Maruizio Lambardi's Brunello. He is a loving and knowledgeable user of the traditional Slavonian durmas oak casks of great capacity, from which he obtains a Brunello with the strong, full flavour of young wine and the balanced and harmonious gentleness of aged wine.

OTHER PRODUCTS

Brunello grappa,
extra virgin olive oil

LE MACIOCHE

LE MACIOCHE
azienda agricola Palazzina
strada provinciale 55 di Sant'Antimo - 53024 Montalcino (Siena)
☎ +39 0577 849168
🖷 +39 0577 849168

Brunello di Montalcino de Le Macioche takes its name from the characteristic and impenetrable wood that overlooks the company, bordering on to the west side.

Acquired without there being any vines or structure in the mid 1980s by a couple of sociable and passionate Roman wine enthusiasts, Matilde Zecca and Achille Mazzocchi, this beautiful holding was totally restructured in only a few years and, later in 1988, 3 hectares of Sangiovese were planted, while in 1995 there was the new launch of the first product label on to the market, from the year 1991.

Subsequent harvests have led to the 2 owners, Matilde and Achille, dedicating themselves to exalting the best of the quality of the grapes produced in four distinctive vineyards, located on the 4 sides of the company's limits (the one looking on to the main road including a hectare of new olive grove).

THE WINES

Brunello di Montalcino docg,
Brunello di Montalcino
docg Riserva,
Rosso di Montalcino doc

The crowning glory of this work is a recently established wine producing cellar which utilises up-to-the-moment architectonic techniques, building being personally followed by the owner, a mechanical engineer. Inside, in the fresh cavern placed under the low hill that houses the company, the vintages of Brunello di Montalcino 'Le Macioche' age in their cloak of dark glass, as well as the Reserves, these last obtainable only for special vintages of selected grapes.

Brunello della Palazzina distinguishes itself very well for its opulent note and for its grand opulent note and for its persistence, being both ample and then balanced, due to the particular exposure of the vineyards, which receive healthy and invigorating lateral breezes from the valleys, useful for avoiding damaging humid stagnation and either excessive heat or cold.

OTHER PRODUCTS

Brunello grappa,
extra virgin olive oil

LA MAGIA

AZIENDA AGRICOLA LA MAGIA
località la Magia - 53024 Montalcino (Siena)
☎ +39 0577 835667
📠 +39 0577 835558
✉ fattorialamagia@tiscali.it

LA MAGIA

The Schwarz family came to the 'la Magia' farm near Montalcino in 1979, attracted by the suggestive panoramas that can be enjoyed from the terraced hill that overlooks the splendid Sant'Antimo Abbacy from the north. Harald Schwarz and his wife Gabriella Zeitler, who come from Merano, gave life to a modern vineyard that produces about forty thousand bottles of Brunello per year today, of which two thousand belong to a 'special' line, labelled annually by contemporary artists. The grapes come from the sixteen hectares of a twenty-five year old vineyard with southern exposure, cultivated with natural methods.

The Schwarz's efforts, which have also been oriented towards the drastic reduction of chemical substances in cultivating the vineyard, have led to more robust and resistant vines, planted in healthy terrain and grapes of extremely high quality. The same principles are respected in the

THE WINES

Brunello di Montalcino docg,
Rosso di Montalcino doc,
Rosato vino da tavola

process of vinification. Alongside the choice to treat the raw material, Sangiovese grosso grapes, in an ecologically sane manner, the vineyard employs technologically advanced systems, albeit in full respect of local tradition.

In addition to the fine job of remodelling done on the large rural home, Harald Schwarz has also built a wine cellar and a large cask cellar, inspired by the most modern techniques of vinification and aging.

The particular octagonal shape of the cellar makes it possible to distribute the fermentation vats in an optimal manner. Many of the fermentation vats are made of wood, the preferred material for the production of an even more interesting Brunello di Montalcino.

Additionally, the various enological processes involved in the construction of the product are very well managed at the 'la Magia' vineyard.

IL MARRONETO

**AZIENDA AGRICOLA IL MARRONETO
di Alessandro Mori**
☞ località Madonna delle Grazie, 307 - 53024 Montalcino (Siena)
☎ +39 0577 849382
🖶 +39 0577 849382
✉ ilmarroneto@ftbcc.it

IL MARRONETO

Producing a wine for passion, during your free time from a different job, may at times reserve pleasant surprises. This is the case of attorney at law Alessandro Mori, who has witnessed the care his family has dedicated to their small estate in Montalcino since he was an adolescent, and decided to dedicate himself exclusively to the production of Brunello, moving the entire family from Siena to the country.

In 1976 the first Sangiovese grapes of the new Marroneto were ready; a little later, after the 1979 harvest, Mori was convinced that he could bottle a worthy product.

He approached Brunello in a manner that rejected all of the enological practices based on harsh corrective methods, which, according to Alessandro Mori, falsify the beauty of Sangiovese, which is potentially 'exasperated' in a positive sense, by the terroir. Working selected grapes, never adding heavy chemical sub-

THE WINES
Brunello di Montalcino docg

stances, after having had the privilege of following the entire evolution of the vineyard – this is the passion of Alessandro, which takes concrete form in his work of continuous control of the fermentation between one barrel and another, re-launching, slowing and nursing the musts with skins, which after a while are separated, to let the wine evolve in the necessary natural manner and without the encumbrance of the liquid with amber tones, which will become Brunello in four year's time.

When it is then packaged in a limited series of bottles, never more than 4,000, the Brunello del Marroneto begins to make its way to the tables and palates of great enthusiasts.

A typical concept that takes its cue and useful elements from common tradition, coupled however with the strong personal artistic sense of the producer.

MASTROJANNI

AZIENDA AGRICOLA MASTROJANNI ss
Podere Loreto San Pio - 53020 Castelnuovo dell'Abate (Siena)
☎ +39 0577 835681
🖷 +39 0577 835505

THE WINES

Brunello di Montalcino docg,
Brunello di Montalcino
docg Riserva,
Brunello di Montalcino docg
'Vigna Schiena d'asino',
Rosso di Montalcino doc,
San Pio igt 'Botrys'

There was nothing but a spectacular panorama and a vast hillside full of fields, woods and olives when, in 1975, attorney at law Gabirele Mastrojanni reached his new land in Montalcino. No vineyard, no cellar, nor water, nor electricity, nor was there a roof on the old ruins he had purchased.

Regardless of his pioneer beginnings, in the portions with the best vocation for vine growing on the 90 hectares of the company, in 1976 11 hectares of vineyard were planted, which became 21 hectares over the years.

Born in the area south east of the territory of Castelnuovo dell'Abate, without large initial investments, the economy of the company rested in the initial years on proceeds from the sale of Brunello: the first balance sheet that came up even was in 1984, after 10 years of commitment to qualify the resources of the company.

Viticulturists and especially inspired winemakers, the Mastrojannis found in Antonio, the founder's son, the representative of the right productive philosophy, based on the awareness of the fortunate situation of succeeding in applying feelings of respect and love for nature in transforming grapes to wine.

The quantity of Brunello marketed annually by Mastrojanni is unforeseeable and changeable. Depending on the vintage, they can go from 15,000 to 45,000 bottles; if the production of Brunello is not considered satisfactory, the grapes are used to produce Rosso doc.

Alongside their traditional line, the Mastrojannis also produce a few thousand bottles of special Brunello, called 'Vigna Schiena d'Asino', because of the particular form of the rocky and sunny hillside, where the best vineyard grows.

PALAGETTO

PALAGETTO srl
⊠ podere Bellarina - 53024 Montalcino (Siena)
☎ +39 0577 943090
🖷 +39 0577 943090
✉ palagetto@iol.it
🖳 www.palagetto.it

THE WINES

Brunello di Montalcino docg,
Brunello di Montalcino
docg Riserva,
Rosso di Montalcino doc

The genealogy of the Sabrina Nic-colai, who runs the Palagetto vineyard together with her husband Mario Fioravanti, is well rooted in a sentiment of love for the land and its fruits. Both of their grandfathers were occupied in the management of the wine cellar in San Gimignano and in the wintertime, her Grandfa-ther Gino also followed the activity of pressing olives for oil.

Therefore, the Niccolai family have always had oil and wine in their heart. When Sabrina and Mario are not busy taking care of their little daughter Arianne, they can often be found supervising one of the com-plex activities involved in managing the five farms of their property, lo-cated in the best winegrowing areas of the region, or supervising some intricate process in the construction of their wines, alongside super enol-ogist Giacomo Tachis, who is a pre-cious consultant of theirs for every quality-oriented vinification.

The 'Bellarina' vineyard was purchased in 1992, where Brunello di Montalcino is produced on the three hectares atop the hills that face Mount Amiata, in Castelnuovo dell'Abate; but a new plantation of two hectares recently came into production, increasing the number of bottles of Brunello and Rosso that will be produced in upcoming harvests.

A production of some 6 or 7 thousand Bordeaux bottles of Brunello is foreseen, and it is a particularly rare event when a harvest is destined to the superior type, Palagetto, which can be produced only with Sangiovese grosso grapes in certain favourable years. It is aged a year longer than normal Brunello, and only a few hundred Bordeaux bottles are turned out, which are made all the more precious by the name Brunello di Montalcino 'Riserva'.

OTHER PRODUCTS

Brunello grappa

PARADISO

AZIENDA AGRICOLA PARADISO
di Mauro Fastelli
☞ località Paradiso, 323 - 53024 Montalcino (Siena)
☎ +39 0577 848250
🖷 +39 0577 848250

The Paradiso vineyard, owned by Mauro Fastelli, was founded in 1965. The first year Brunello di Montalcino was produced was 1979, when some 15,000 bottles were turned out. The area of cultivation covers five hectares of vineyards out of a total of 6.5 hectares, with 3.000 m² planted in olive groves.

Mauro Fastelli, whose family has lived in Montalcino for generations, was among the founders of the Consortium of Protection for Brunello wine in 1967, and has dedicated much of his time to consortium activities since that time, to ennoble the activity of small vineyards, like his own, who had long been working to cut themselves out a niche in the market, in the face of competition from the large Ilcinese historical estates.

The Paradise vineyard is well integrated in the precious surroundings of its natural environment; the cellar is underground and the main body

THE WINES
Brunello di Montalcino docg,
Rosso di Montalcino doc,
Vin Santo

of the company, which dates from the thirties, was recently restructured with knowing skill.

Even if one of Fastelli's passions is the Tuscan product par excellence, the famous Vin Santo, to which he dedicates much of his care in the cellar, the vinification of Brunello grapes obviously remains the principle objective of the company.

The vineyards are oriented towards the northeast, on a terrace that forms the base of the Ilcinese hill.

The grapes in this sub zone of Brunello are therefore less sugary and not overcome by the boiling breath of the Mediterranean, which thus makes the wine from this land fresher and more acid, which is a sign of good potential for aging. Fastelli's Brunello therefore assumes a certain elegance of structure, amplified as it is by exuberant perfumes.

OTHER PRODUCTS

Brunello grappa,
extra virgin olive oil

LA PESCAIA

AZIENDA AGRICOLA DI DONATO a.r.v.e.
LA PESCAIA
📧 località la Pescaia - 53024 Montalcino (Siena)
☎ +39 0577 847185
📠 +39 0577 847185

In the archives of the City of Montalcino, transactions are recorded involving vineyards, starting from the third century, with property changing hands in vine growing areas. Indicated in these registrations with the term 'vineyard' which defines a united parcel situated around the principal urban centres of the area, is the Pescaia, a locality that has been producing wine since the year one thousand.

This area, set on the step-shaped hillside underneath the town of Montalcino, in the direction of the Arbia Valley, along the road to Buonconvento, has represented Ilcinese wine since its birth.

It does not surprise us therefore, that thanks to this pedigree, Brunello from the Pescaia often receives flattering comments in specialised guides. Today the vineyard has a total of 15 hectares, eight of which are dedicated to the cultivation of Sangiovese, and six of which are ear-

THE WINES

Brunello di Montalcino docg,
Rosso di Montalcino doc,
Rosso Sant'Antimo doc,
Rosso Val d'Orcia doc

marked for the creation of Brunello and two for Rosso. The first year Brunello di Montalcino was produced at the Pescaia was 1985. The vineyard located halfway down the hillside, on a terrain of average consistency, made up of clay, sand and clay shale, with a barbed cord planting system that takes the stalks to a height of 80 cm from the ground, with a planting density of between 3.300 and 4.500 vines per hectare.

The land had belonged to the Mantengoli family since 1870, until the company recently changed hands, becoming one of the wine growing firms of the dynamic brothers Aniceto, Enzo, Roberto and Vittorio Di Donato, who originally come from the area around Val d'Orcia, where they were already winegrowers, but, rightly so, they wanted to maintain the characteristics of 'true' Brunello, following in the footsteps of the previous owners.

OTHER PRODUCTS

Brunello grappa,
extra virgin olive oil

PIAN DELL'ORINO

PIAN DELL'ORINO
di Pobitzer Caroline
☞ località Pian dell'Orino - 53024 Montalcino (Siena)
☎ +39 0577 849301
🖷 +39 0577 849301
✉ caroline@piandellorino.it
🖥 www.piandellorino.it

THE WINES
Brunello di Montalcino docg,
Rosso di Montalcino doc,
Orellino vdt, Piandorino igt

Caroline Pobitzer moved to the Sienese territory and bottled her first Brunello in the mythical year of 1997, on a tract of land purchased in the eastern area of the Montalcino hillside.

It was hard times for her when, together with the reconstruction of the rural house located at the centre of the parcel of land she had purchased, the re-qualification of the old vineyards turned out to be equally expensive, in a clay shale and hostile terrain. She was fortunate enough to plant 5 hectares of vineyard, all of them with Sangiovese, on terrain that bordered the oldest Brunello vineyard, the Greppo, interpreting this mythical terroir in a very personal manner.

She is the daughter of a noble family of Meranese winegrowers, who own a vine that is 600 years old (probably the oldest vine in the world), she transferred the magnificent atmosphere of her Upper Adige castle in Prissiano, between Merano and Bolzano, to the sweet Ilcinese Terraces, finding herself here in the company of other illustrious countrymen, winegrowers who have obtained honorary Tuscan citizenship.

Caroline Pobitzer cultivates the Tuscan vine par excellence, Sangiovese grosso, otherwise known as Brunello, together with the young German enologist Jan Erbach, utilising biological methods, and obtains from her grapes a wine processed to yield great freshness and taste.

Almost all of the terrain given over to vine growing on the Orino Plain is registered in the Brunello roll of Montalcino docg, and from the most recent plantations, of little more than a hectare, a fine Rosso di Montalcino doc can be obtained at will, or a Sant'Antimo Sangiovese doc.

PIAN DI MACINA

AZIENDA AGRICOLA PIAN DI MACINA
di Marco Tempori
localitá Pian di macina - 53024 Montalcino (Siena)
☎ +39 0577 849035
🖷 +39 0577 849035
💻 pdm@piandimacina.it
🖳 www.piandimacina.it

The history of Pian di Macina is the same as many other small vineyards, which have produced wine to be sold without bottling or to bring to age in casks of larger vineyards.

It was Bruno Sassetti, at the beginning of the sixties, who created this firm, which is very near the centre of Montalcino, hidden on the hill that goes down towards the suburb of Torrenieri, on the east side of the city territory. Today the work of building the vineyards has continued through his grandson Marco, owner of the firm, together with his mother Graziella. They avail themselves of the assistance of Luciano, Marco's father.

About half of the 5 hectares of land given over to Brunello vineyard were planted recently and release their grapes with parsimony, given their young age. The remaining 2.5 hectares already produce fine grapes, all Sangiovese, which the

THE WINES
Brunello di Montalcino docg,
Rosso di Montalcino doc

rare bottles with the Pian di Macina initials presented for the first time on the market in 1997.

Initially assisted by a local enologist, Roberto Bruchi, the Temporis express in their wine the passion for a tradition that is respected in its most genuine and fundamental traits. No contamination is allowed in the various vintages of Brunello, the vineyard and newly planted vines are worked as they once were, with no technologically advanced aids applied to the vinification.

The yeasts are autochthonous and rigorously come from the same material as the company grapes, with an absolute predilection for large durmast oak casks. Thus, the Brunello of the Pian di Macina is presented on the market with an extremely special taste, a considerably powerful component of alcohol and a fine quality-price ratio.

IL POGGIOLO

IL POGGIOLO
località il Poggiolo, 259 - 53024 Montalcino (Siena)
+39 0577 848412
+39 0577 848412
www.ilpoggiolomontalcino.com

THE WINES

Brunello di Montalcino docg,
Brunello di Montalcino
docg Riserva,
Brunello di Montalcino
docg 'Beato', Brunello
di Montalcino docg 'Sassello',
Brunello di Montalcino
docg 'Terrarossa',
Rosso di Montalcino
doc 'Sassello',
Rosso di Montalcino doc
'Terrarossa',
Bottaccio Toscana igt,
Concreto, In riva al fosso igt
'Toscana', Oltre,
Sasso nero igt 'Toscana'

Roberto Cosimi started producing Brunello in 1971. In the years immediately following its founding, the Poggiolo farm had time to grow and establish its presence in the territory, vinifying Brunello grapes from 4 hectares of vineyards.

Rodolfo Cosimo, who is called Rudy by his friends, has been addressing production towards extremely elevated standards of quality since 1984. Rudy is the one who has maintained the prestige of his father's wines high, by hypothesizing and realising a system of selection that allows the firm to market three diffrent types of Brunello, each from the grapes of a specific vineyard, with a view to emulating the French cru.

The first barriques appeared in his cellar as early as the nineties, when experimentation was being carried out on toasting procedures and in connection with the geographical origin of different woods, the purpose of which was to apply the knowledge acquired to the various lines of selected production.

The systems of vinification therefore go hand in hand with this productive philosophy, and the care taken in fermentation time, equipment and aging techniques takes concrete form under three labels: vintage Brunello, 'Brunello Beato' and 'Brunello Sassello'.

According to Rudy the true characteristic of the firm is to make every Brunello vineyard different, to exalt to the utmost the potential of the land in each area cultivated by the company. The number of bottles produced in each of the three lines varies according to the progress of the season. The Sassello cru is produced only in exceptional years, while about two thousand bottles of the Beato are produced annually and rigorously packaged in numbered six-bottle cases.

OTHER PRODUCTS

Brunello grappa,
Brunello brandy

IL POGGIONE

TENUTA IL POGGIONE
di Leopoldo e Livia Franceschi ss
✉ Sant'Angelo in Colle - 53024 Montalcino (Siena)
☎ +39 0577 844029
🖹 +39 0577 844165
✉ ilpoggione@tin.it
🖥 www.tenutailpoggione.it

IL POGGIONE

THE WINES

Brunello di Montalcino docg,
Brunello di Montalcino docg
'Riserva il Poggione',
Moscadello di Montalcino doc,
Rosso di Montalcino doc,
Rosso Toscana igt,
San Leopoldo Toscana igt,
Vin Santo,
Sant'Antimo doc

The Poggione estate has been the property of the Franceschi family since the nineteenth century, which makes it one of the historical companies in the territory.

Confirmation of the suitability of the area to produce superior quality wines and the challenge of Sangiovese and its Brunello started in the Lavinio Franceschi vineyard, whose ideal witnesses today are its current proprietors, Leopoldo and Livia Franceschi, assisted in the management of the company by the agronomist and enologist Fabrizio Bindocci, who has been in their employee for 25 years.

Leopoldo Franceschi proudly asserts that his father and his grandfather before him had always taught him that great red wines are obtained in the vineyard, the only way to produce superior quality grapes. For this reason, he continues to carry forward with love and passion the care for the vineyards and the choice of the best clones, always, however in full respect of Brunello's typical nature.

The Poggione is today one of the largest vitiviniculture companies in Montalcino, with 108 hectares of specialised vineyard, of which 60 are cultivated with Sangiovese grapes for the production of Brunello.

The enormous quantity of light and air that benefit the vineyards, thanks to their exposition on the Sant'Angelo hillside, which, being open at all altitudes, allows ideal maturation for the grapes produced there.

From the area known as the 'Paganelli', a 40 year old vineyard, a particular Brunello Reserve known as 'il Poggione' is produced in great vintage years. This reserve develops its aromas for 36 months in Allier durmast oak casks, then rests for another 12 months in the bottle before going to market.

OTHER PRODUCTS
Brunello grappa,
extra virgin olive oil

TIEZZI

AZIENDA AGRICOLA ENZO TIEZZI
via delle Querce, 5 - 53024 Montalcino (Siena)
☎ +39 0577 848187
📠 +39 0577 848187

THE WINES
Brunello di Montalcino docg,
Rosso di Montalcino doc,
Sant'Antimo doc Bianco,
Cerrino Toscana igt

Enzo Tiezzi has built his beautiful new vineyard starting from a great passion, first of all for his native land, and secondly for its most representative product, Brunello di Montalcino, obviously.

After dedicating years in civil service, as Consortium President and wine cellar technician for other blazoned vineyards, Tiezzi, who is a kind, well prepared and cultured man, decided to produce his wine in the shadow of tradition.

In his case it was therefore not a problem of using this or that method of vinification, but of faithfully rebuilding what was perhaps the first historical vineyard of Montalcino, the Soccorso vineyard, which had for centuries been cultivated right under the city cathedral, and was celebrated for having been the property of one of the discoverers of Brunello, Riccardo Paccagnini. Great care was taken in recovering the old farmhouse, to conserve all of the architectural peculiarities and reproduce a model of the home that was as close to possible as the age-old original.

Outside the vineyard was replanted with the 'small tree' system, the terraces were rebuilt and Enzo Tiezzi replanted old fruit orchards here and there, which produced such delicious fruit and were historically part of the Tuscan countryside. The capable and ecological winegrower even succeeded in bringing in electric wires and telephone cables without the slightest contamination of the environment.

If that isn't love for nature...

Today, at the Soccorso and other vineyards that he owns or rents, Tiezzi produces 25,000 bottles of Brunello di Montalcino, previously aged for the three canonical years in large durmast oak casks.

OTHER PRODUCTS

Brunello grappa

LA TORRE

AZIENDA AGRICOLA LA TORRE
di Luigi Anania
✉ località la Torre - 53024 Montalcino (Siena)
☎ +39 0577 844073
🖷 +39 0577 847151
✉ luigi.anania@libero.it

THE WINES

Brunello di Montalcino docg,
Brunello di Montalcino
docg Riserva,
Rosso di Montalcino doc

Luigi Anania, the enologist, earned his degree in agrarian science in 1976, with a thesis that analysed the quality of the Brunello di Montalcino produced by vineyards of different dimensions.

A year later he decided to purchase a vineyard that covered thirty-six hectares, in the area to the south of Montalcino, on the hills that dominate the Orcia Valley, just a few paces from Sant'Angelo in Colle.

From 1977 to 1999, in the best terrains the Torre farm had to offer, he made several plantations of vineyards. Today these plantations extend over a surface of six hectares, which are entirely given over to the Sangiovese vine.

The presence of vineyards of different ages allows Luigi Anania to select and verify, year after year, the potential structure and aging of his wines, which he wishes to exalt above all by enhancing their body, thanks also to the particular pedoclimactic conditions of this typically Mediterranean area, which is considered the 'Sicily' of the Brunello region.

Another characteristic that makes Brunello della Torre interesting is the general harmony and perfumes, which are obtained thanks to the selection of grapes used to produce the wine, which remain extremely fresh thanks to the high altitude of the plantation.

Added to a method of vinification considered *"traditional but not conservative"*, being Ananìa's own definition, – which foresees the limited use of small carats, prefering to use large durmast oak casks from Slavonia – are the low environmental impact agronomical practices implemented by Ananìa, who carefully studies the correct use of fertilisers, which are used with the intention of determining the optimum structure of the grapes grown in the vineyards involved.

UCCELLIERA

AZIENDA AGRICOLA UCCELLIERA
di Andrea Cortonesi
podere Uccelliera, 45 - 53020 Castelnuovo dell'Abate (Siena)
☎ +39 0577 835729
📠 +39 0577 835729
✉ anco@uccelliera-montalcino.it
🖥 www.uccelliera-montalcino.it

The objective of Andrea Cortonesi, proprietor of the Uccelliera company, a vined parcel to the south east of Montalcino, is to contribute concretely to realising the best with his vinification that nature is capable of offering in this fertile land.

Uccelliera is the original name of the farmhouse, with the annexed agricultural terrain, that Cortonesi purchased in 1986 and transformed into a vineyard and wine cellar for the production and refining of Brunello di Montalcino.

But respect for the traditional physiognomy of this suggestive area has inspired the new proprietor to plant olive groves as well, alongside the precious vines.

The latter cover six hectares, have a high density of plants and are made up of selected Sangiovese clones.

Andrea Cortonesi understands the enological aspect not as a manipulation that man carries out on

THE WINES
Brunello di Montalcino docg,
Rosso di Montalcino doc,
Rapace Toscana igt

grapes, but as a well-aimed intervention, faithful to the genuine expression of the innate characteristics that may be expressed by the territory.

It is to this intervention, in producing a great wine, that the potential of the vine must be tied, which expresses itself in that particular territory, as well as the traditional care taking of man.

As a supporter of the need for a close synergy between the winegrowers and the denomination itself, whether they are large or small producers, the proprietor of the Uccelliera looks with caution upon the exasperated use of wood when it is used to change the wine.

Wood is useful to refine and balance the sensorial characteristics of the wine, but it should not be used to override the original qualities that it has developed, unwarrantedly conditioning its taste.

OTHER PRODUCTS
Brunello grappa,
extra virgin olive oil

VILLA LE PRATA

AZIENDA AGRICOLA VILLA LE PRATA
di Benedetta Losappio
✉ via Castiglion del bosco, 261 - 53024 Montalcino (Siena)
☎ +39 0577 848325
🖷 +39 0577 848325
✉ alcoyle@tin.it
🖵 www.villaleprata.com

VILLA LE PRATA

THE WINES

Brunello di Montalcino docg,
Rosso di Montalcino
doc 'Tirso',
Rosso Le Prata igt 'Toscana'

The headquarters of Villa Le Prata is a majestic building, built in 1862 by Count Carlo de Vecchi as a shooting lodge for hunting, to host notables visiting Montalcino.

In 1982, the Losappio family came into the possession of the lodge and in the following years they laid the basis for the organisation of a viticulture company set up to produce quality wine, which was managed above all by the women in the family, of whom Benedetta is the current representative.

The first hectare of Sangiovese was planted in 1989. Currently the vineyard has 2 hectares of Brunello and a third hectare that is almost ready to enter into production.

The terrain where the vineyard is planted is arranged around the villa and other buildings in the area of Castel-nuovo dell'Abate. Its two geographical areas are affected by the favourable climactic conditions and guarantee the homogeneous ripening of the grape bunches, which benefit from the protection from the cold northern winds and an altitude of 300 m a.s.l.

The Brunello is produced in small quantities, of about 4,000 bottles per year, and is obviously made up of 100% Sangiovese grosso, and the harvesting is done entirely by hand. A selection of grape bunches guarantees the product has high parameters of quality. The must is fermented in steel vats for about twenty days at controlled temperatures, with remixing three or four times per day.

The wine is then refined in Slavonian durmast oak casks for four years, as foreseen by the regulations, and finishes aging in French 5-hectolitre oak tonneaux, for about twelve months, before finishing its course in the classical heavy Bordeaux bottles.

OTHER PRODUCTS
Brunello grappa

The purpose of the foregoing company profiles is to give the reader a general idea of the production of Brunello di Montalcino. The companies are not listed in any order of merit and the list is entirely subjective.

Our heartfelt thanks go to the companies listed here, who have had faith in this editorial project of ours and assisted us in its realisation.

other producers of Brunello di Montalcino

Abbadia Ardenga (Torrenieri)
Agostina Pieri (Castelnuovo dell'Abate)
Agricola Centolami (Montalcino)
Armilla (Montalcino)
Baricci (Montalcino)
Bellaria (Montalcino)
Brunelli Gianni (Montalcino)
Campana (Montalcino)
Campogiovanni (Sant'Angelo in Colle)
Canalicchio (Montalcino)
Canneta (Montalcino)
Cantina di Montalcino (Montalcino)
Cantine Luciani 1888 (Montalcino)
Capanna (Montalcino)
Capanne Ricci (Sant'Angelo in Colle)
Caprili (Montalcino)
Casanova di Neri (Torrenieri)
Casanuova delle Cerbaie (Montalcino)
Case basse (Montalcino)
Castelgiocondo (Montalcino)

Castelli Martinozzi (Montalcino)
Castello di Monastero (Montalcino)
Castiglion del Bosco (Montalcino)
Cerbaia (Montalcino)
Cerbaiona (Montalcino)
le Chiuse (Torrenieri)
Col di Sole (Montalcino)
Colle (Torrenieri)
Collemattoni (Sant'Angelo in Colle)
Collosorbo (Castelnuovo dell'Abate)
Comunali (Montalcino)
le Crete (Montalcino)
Croce (Montalcino)
Crocedimezzo (Montalcino)
Cupano (Montalcino)
Donna Olga (Montalcino)
Fattoi (Montalcino)
Ferro (Montalcino)
Fiorita (Castelnuovo dell'Abate)
Fornace (Montalcino)

Fornacella (Montalcino)
Fornacina (Torrenieri)
Fortuna (Montalcino)
Fuligni (Montalcino)
Gerla (Montalcino)
Gode (Montalcino)
Gorelli (Montalcino)
Grappolo - Fortius (Sant'Angelo in Colle)
Greppino (Montalcino)
Lecciaia (Montalcino)
Lisini (Montalcino)
la Mannella (Montalcino)
Marchesato degli Aleràmici (Montalcino)
Marchetti (Montalcino)
Mocali (Montalcino)
Molinari Carlo (Montalcino)
Natalini (Montalcino)
Pacenti e Ripaccioli (Montalcino)
Padelletti (Montalcino)
Palazzetta (Castelnuovo dell'Abate)
Palazzo (Montalcino)
Palazzone (Montalcino)
Paradiso di Manfredi (Montalcino)
Paradisone (Montalcino)
Patrizio (Sant'Angelo in Colle)
Pertimali (Montalcino)
Piancornello (Castelnuovo dell'Abate)
Pian delle vigne (Montalcino)
Pietroso (Montalcino)
Pieve di san Sigismondo (Montalcino)
Pieve santa Restituta (Montalcino)
Pinino (Montalcino)
Poderina - Saiagricola (Castelnuovo dell'Abate)
Poderuccio (Sant'Angelo in Colle)
Poggiarellino (Montalcino)
Poggio antico (Montalcino)
Poggio il Castellare (Castelnuovo dell'Abate)
Poggio san Polo (Montalcino)
Poggio di sotto (Castelnuovo dell'Abate)

Poggio degli ulivi (Castelnuovo dell'Abate)
Presi (Castelnuovo dell'Abate)
Quercecchio (Montalcino)
Rasina (Montalcino)
Riguardo (Montalcino)
Rogarelli (Montalcino)
Salicutti (Montalcino)
Salvioni (Montalcino)
San Carlo (Montalcino)
San Filippo (Montalcino)
San Giorgio (Castelnuovo Abate)
Santa Giulia (Torrenieri)
Santa Maria (Montalcino)
Sassetti (Montalcino)
Sassetti Vasco (Castelnuovo dell'Abate)
Scopetino (Montalcino)
Scopetone (Montalcino)
Serena (Torrenieri)
Sesta di sopra (Castelnuovo dell'Abate)
Sesti (Sant'Angelo in Colle)
Siro Pacenti (Montalcino)
Solaria (Montalcino)
Talenti (Sant'Angelo in Colle)
Tenimenti Angelini - Val di Suga (Montalcino)
Tenimenti Natalini (Montalcino)
Tenuta Caparzo (Torrenieri)
Tenuta la Fuga (Montalcino)
Tenuta Greppone Mazzi (Montalcino)
Tenuta di Sesta (Castelnuovo dell'Abate)
Tenuta Oliveto (Montalcino)
Tenute Silvio Nardi (Montalcino)
Togata (Montalcino)
Tornesi (Montalcino)
Valdicava (Montalcino)
Verbena (Montalcino)
Vigna (Montalcino)
Villa Poggio Salvi (Montalcino)
Villa a Tolli (Montalcino)
Vitanza (Montalcino)

CONSORZIO DEL VINO BRUNELLO DI MONTALCINO

Costa del Municipio, 1 - 53024 Montalcino (Siena)
TELEPHONE 0577 848246
FAX 0577 849425
E-MAIL consbrun@tin.it
WEBSITE www.consorziobrunellodimontalcino.it

A gastronomical tour of the land of Brunello

Until now you have read everything that could have been written about Brunello di Montalcino and its lovely lands, home to the vineyards. We have talked about wine, its characteristic bouquet and its robust and tannic flavour, speaking also about the producers who dedicate their time and passion. But the Brunello lands are also home to other tastes and fragrances, discovered through the enjoyable pointers contained here within. Have a nice trip 'enjoying', in fact…

costa Castellare, 1-3 - 53020 Sant'Angelo in Colle (Siena)
telephone +39 0577 844175 - fax +39 0577 844176
laurafregoli@iol.it

ristorante BANFI

The Banfi restaurant is situated in an old castle from the 11th century. Guido Haverkock, the chef, is the creator of sought after dishes, such as the thyme *risotto with little dry tomatoes and goat's cheese, bass with potato savoury pie, potato gnocchi with guinea fowl sauce* and *saddle of roe with lard and pomegranate sauce.*

località Colombio Tozzi, 201 - 53024 Montalcino (Siena)
telephone +39 0577 848233 - fax +39 0577 846570
www.bsur.it/boccondivino

ristorante BOCCON DI VINO

Mario Fiorani, supported in the kitchen by his wife Vanna and daughters Marina and Alessandra, offers the reworking of traditional dishes in his establishment, such as the *traditional 'peposo'*, the *'carrabaccia'* and *boar 'scottiglia'*, as well as the creation of new dishes, like *tortelloni with saffron and truffles.*

località Bellaria - 53024 Montalcino (Siena)
telephone +39 0577 849304 - fax +39 0577 849430
www.hotelalbrunello.it

ristorante AL BRUNELLO DI MONTALCINO

The Bartolomei family offers *'pinci' pasta with bread-crumbs, bread soup, 'pappardelle' pasta with wild boar sauce* and *'tagliatelle' pasta with 'porcino' mushrooms* and *potato gnocchi*, all at their hotel restaurant. For the second course they offer *Montalcino tripe, alpine fillet, wild boar 'scottiglia'* and *Florentine steak*. For dessert, *apple pie.*

località Velona - 53024 Castelnuovo dell'Abate (Siena)
telephone +39 0577 800101 - fax +39 0577 835661
www.castellodivelona.it

ristorante CASTELLO DI VELONA

The Castello di Velona restaurant places the castle at the disposition of clients: in addition to the breathtaking view, pool and comfortable suites, an ever changing 'territory based' menu is on offer from the restaurant kitchen, with *'tagliatella' pasta with chianina ragout sauce, braised beef al Brunello, Florentine steak* and *'pinolata'.*

località Podernuovi, 170 - 53024 Montalcino (Siena)
telephone +39 0577 841200 - fax +39 0577 841112
www.fattoriadeibarbi.it

ristorante TAVERNA DEI BARBI

This restaurant, annexed to the cellar of the Cinelli Colombini family, serves traditional Tuscan cuisine, such as *'pinci' pasta with ragout sauce,* '*porcino' mushroom soup, 'stracotto' meat with Vin Santo, braised beef with Brunello, wild boar 'scottiglia'* and the splendid *cheeses* and *salami* produced by the company.

piazza Cavour, 1 - 53024 Montalcino (Siena)
telephone +39 0577 849076
fax +39 0577 849076

osteria AL GIARDINO

Gianluca serves his offerings in characteristic earthenware plates. The pasta is hand made: *pinci, pappardelle, ravioli* and *gnocchi*. There is also *rice with chicory and sheep's cheese, Etruscan style rabbit, wild boar 'poacher style'* and the *fine meat loaf, Moscadello 'stracotto'* and *leg of piglet al Brunello*.

Scale di via Moglio, 1 - 53024 Montalcino (Siena)
telephone +39 0577 847150 - fax +39 0577 846400
www.grappoloblu.it

ristorante GRAPPOLO BLU

This spot has the atmosphere of old hostelries, or inns, where one can eat and drink well, choosing from 350 labels. In the kitchen we have Maria Pia, helped in the dining room by her husband Luciano. The *ravioli with sheep's cheese* are excellent, as are the *'crostini'*, *'pinci' pasta with garlic* and *rabbit with Brunello*.

piazza il Pozzo - 53020 Sant'Angelo in Colle (Siena)
telephone +39 0577 844015
fax +39 0577 844076

trattoria IL POZZO

In the medieval township, tasty fragrances are on offer in Paola and Franca Binarelli's little trattoria restaurant. Fragrances that spill out on to the streets. The offerings are *onion soup*, *'pinci' pasta with breadcrumbs*, *chicken 'scottiglia'*, *bread soup*, *tasty portions of beef al Brunello*, *rabbit with onions* and *fruit pies*.

via Giacomo Matteotti, 15 - 53024 Montalcino (Siena)
telephone +39 0577 847054 - fax +39 0577 847054
enotecabacchusmontalcino@yahoo.it

enoteca BACCHUS

Isabella and Ezio Pompanin sell typical Tuscan produce in their wine shop, such as *Pienza sheep's cheese*, also with truffle aroma, wild game *cold meats* (boar, roe and deer) as well as the Sienese cinta, *extra virgin olive oil* and *honey*. At the table you may taste all of these by matching them with a good selection of wines.

località Fontepetri - 53024 Montalcino (Siena)
telephone +39 0577 806241 - fax +39 0577 806241
fontepetri@libero.it

wine shop-enoteca FONTEPETRI

Three hectares with a farmhouse make up the agriturismo restaurant of Domenico and Francesca, spouses with a passion for hospitality and wine. In addition to the possibility of booking one of the lovely apartments, there are fine *wines*, *honeys*, *oils* and *'pinci' pasta* in the wine shop, the heart of the company.

piazzale Fortezza - 53024 Montalcino (Siena)
telephone +39 0577 829211
fortezza@enoteccalafortezza.it - www.enotecalafortezza.it

enoteca LA FORTEZZA DI MONTALCINO

This restaurant is located inside the Montalcino fortress. Along with the *cold meats, cheeses, oil* and *honeys* (strawberry trees, acacia and chestnut), there is a collection of different types of *Brunello*. You can sit at table, eating the local cold meat salami and cheese products, combined with the wines.

piazzale Fortezza, 5 - 53024 Montalcino (Siena)
telephone +39 0577 848191 - fax +39 0577 849077
www.enotecafranci.com

enoteca FRANCI

Fabio Tassi and his wife Manola competently offer a wide selection of Ilcinese wines in this, their second wine shop, without forgetting the best international labels. Next to the *wines*, there is an ample selection of *honey* (home made), *jams, biscuits, 'pinci' pasta* and *local sweets.*

costa di piazza Garibaldi, 3 - 53024 Montalcino (Siena)
telephone +39 0577 848095 - fax +39 0577 847117
grottadelbrunello@tin.it

enoteca GROTTA DEL BRUNELLO

Giancarlo Luciani has transformed an old Ilcinese cellar (where at one time wine, flowing from the cask, was sold) into a wine shop where the *Brunello grappa* has a room dedicated all to itself, where the *wines* are only Tuscan and where you lose yourself among *honey* jars, *pasta, extra virgin olive oil* and *jams.*

costa di piazza Garibaldi, 3 - 53024 Montalcino (Siena)
telephone +39 0577 849418 - fax +39 0577 849418
enoteca@montalcinoproduce.it

enoteca MONTALCINO PRODUCE

Gigliola Gorelli, owner of this wine shop, a dynamic lady knowledgeable about *wine*, proposes a fine selection of Tuscan and non-Tuscan wines to her clientele, bottles keeping company in shopping bags with *grappa, honey, marmalade, jams* and Tuscan *extra virgin olive oil.*

piazza del Popolo, 16 - 53024 Montalcino (Siena)
telephone +39 0577 849113 - fax +39 0577 849113
enotecapierangioli@hotmail.com

enoteca PIERANGIOLI

Sergio Pierangioli is custodian of the jewels of Bacchus. He moves with mastery among the hundreds of labels of the best Tuscan wines, with Brunello at the head of the pack. Among the shelves of bottles you find *extra virgin olive oil, pasta, honey, jam, dried mushrooms* and *aromatic herbs* for cooking.

vicolo del Vecchietta, 5 - 53027 San Quirico d'Orcia (Siena)
telephone +39 0577 897726
www.crocusbrandi.it

zafferano ANTONIO BRANDI

The *Crocus* flower contains the saffron, a substance that is well loved by gourmets and appreciated in the kitchen too. Egisto Brandi, cultivator, is the alchemist of saffron, selling it in *pistils* or in *pads of butter*. You can also book delicious meals crowned with saffron, prepared by his wife.

via della Madonnina, 38 - 53026 Pienza (Siena)
telephone +39 0578 748097 - fax +39 0578 748760
clubnaturista@tiscalinet.it

prodotti tipici CLUB DEL NATURISTA

Two hearts for one biologist: Antonio and Maria Laura Pignatello, husband and wife in their company dispensary, present a rich array of Aiab certified products, with *pasta* (al Brunello too), *honey, biscuits* and the *non-alcoholic digestive liquors* (with rhubarb and mixed herbs).

via Grossetana, 19 - 53024 Sant'Angelo Scalo (Siena)
telephone +39 0577 808006 - fax +39 0577 808006
eleonora.pieri@virgilio.it

macelleria e norcineria CARLO PIERI

Even the most hard-core vegetarian, on entering Carlo Pieri and wife Milva's bottega, would simply remark: *"well, perhaps just a little piece"*. In addition to the best cuts of *Chianina meat* and *pork*, they also offer *cold hams, porchetta ham, cheek, finocchione, sausages, salamis* and...

via Bellaria, 10 - 53024 Montalcino (Siena)
telephone +39 0577 848414
fax +39 0577 848414

enoteca LES BARRIQUES

In Montalcino's main street we find Guido and Marco Martini's and Gigliola Monaci's wine shop, frequented by those who stop for a glass of wine and by those who sit down at the table to restore themselves with a typical dish. As well as Tuscan *wines*, you can get *extra virgin olive oil, pasta, honey, cheeses* and *salamis*.

via Soccorso Saloni, 35 - 53024 Montalcino (Siena)
telephone +39 0577 849408 - fax +39 0577 849408
www.kaffeina.org

wine-bar KAFFEINA

This beautiful spot with its post-modern atmosphere is extremely well frequented as a place to drink a fine aperitif. The bar displays salted goodies to accompany cocktails and aperitifs, prepared by Roberto and his daughter Alice. Live music enliven the atmosphere.

Bibliography

AA.VV., *'Buon vino, favola lunga - vite e vino nei proverbi delle regioni italiane'*, Electa e Verona Fiere per il XXVI Vinitaly, Perugia 1992

AA.VV., *'Vino e nutrizione fra storia e antropologia'* (a cura di Luciano Bonuzzi), Consorzio tutela vini Soave e Recioto di Soave, Soave (Verona) 1991

AA.VV., *'L'Amiata e la val d'Orcia - la storia, l'architettura, l'arte delle città e del territorio, itinerari nel patrimonio storico e religioso'*, Mondadori editore e Regione Toscana, Milano 1999

AA.VV., *'Le crete senesi, la val d'Arbia e la val di Merse - la storia, l'architettura, l'arte delle città e del territorio, itinerari nel patrimonio storico e religioso'*, Mondadori editore e Regione Toscana, Milano 1999

AA.VV., *'Montalcino'*, Editrice le Balze, Montepulciano (Siena) 1995

AA.VV., *'L'arte del vino in terra di Toscana'*, Giunti editore, Prato 1994

AA.VV., *'Il paese del vino - guida ai vini doc e docg'*, Enoteca italiana, Siena 2001

AA.VV., *'Vini di Toscana'*, Regione Toscana - Dipartimento agricoltura e foreste - Enoteca italiana di Siena e Editrice Toscanaverde, Firenze 1989

AA.VV., *'Guida pratica agli alberi e arbusti in Italia'*, Selezione del Reader's Digest, Milano 1982

AA.VV., *'Le uve dei Medici'*, Palazzo dei vini, Firenze 1992

AA.VV., *'Il vino degli antichi - la Toscana e il Mediterraneo'*, Palazzo dei vini, Firenze 1992

AA.VV., *'Vino e olio in Toscana'*, Casa editrice il Fiore, Firenze 1988

AA.VV., *'Montalcino e Montepulciano - Val d'Orcia e dintorni'*, Slow food editore, Bra (Cuneo) 2001

AA.VV., *'Anthimiana'*, Edizioni sant'Antimo, Castelnuovo dell'Abate (Siena) 1999

AA.VV., *'Una pietra che canta'*, Edizioni sant'Antimo, Castelnuovo dell'Abate (Siena) 2001

ARDITO STEFANO, *'Un approdo felice - guida alla natura, alla storia e ai segreti del monte Amiata'*, Azienda di promozione turistica dell'Amiata, Abbadia san Salvatore (Siena 1994)

BAGNOLI ALESSANDRO, *'Museo civico e diocesano d'arte sacra di Montalcino'*, edizioni Cantagalli, Siena 1997

BALDINI NICOLETTA, CHERUBINI GIOVANNI, *'Toscana, nuovo millennio - cultura, percorsi, eventi per il Giubileo e oltre'*, Edifir edizioni Firenze, Firenze 1999

BERETTA MARIA CRISTINA, STECCHI GUIDO, *'Guida alle cantine e ai vini d'Italia'*, Mondadori, Milano 2001

BLAISE DE MONLUC, *'All'assedio di Siena e in Montalcini (1554-1557) - a cura di Mario Filippone'*, Edizioni Cantagalli e Nuova Immagine editrice, Siena 1992

BOCCI ZEFFIRO, *'L'evoluzione del settore vitivinicolo negli ultimi trent'anni'*, edizione a cura del Gruppo italiano vini, Bussolengo (Verona) 1997

BOCELLI SAVERIO (a cura di), *'La vite e il vino nell'araldica civica italiana'*, Centro Studi vite e vino Montespertoli e Giampiero Pagnini editore, Firenze 1995

BONUCCI BRUNO, *'Montalcino, pietre e storia'*, Editrice Don Chisciotte, San Quirico d'Orcia (Siena) 1999

CAPRIOLI IVO, PIGNATTAI ASSUNTO, 'Montalcino, diecimila anni di vita alla luce dei ritrovamenti archeologici - ricordi di un'esperienza archeologica', Comitato ricerche e studi etruschi ed italici, Montalcino (Siena) 1994

CARLE LUCIA, DI LELLO LUCIANO, MAZZONI GIANNI, 'Montalcino', Consorzio del vino Brunello di Montalcino, Siena 1998

CERNILLI DANIALE, SABELLICO MARCO, 'Il vino, storia e curiosità', Gambero Rosso Editore, Roma 1994

CIACCI MARIO, 'La torre nera - Torrenieri in Montalcino, la via Francigena, il paese, la campagna', Mario Ciacci, Siena 1999

CLINANTI PINO, 'Il fuoco, il vetro e il vino', Fondazione Villa Banfi, Montalcino (Siena) 1992

CODACCI LEO, 'Civiltà della tavola contadina in Toscana', Idealibri, Rimini 1996

JOHNSON HUGH, 'Il vino - storia, tradizioni, cultura', Franco Muzzio editore, Cuneo 1992

MANCINI MARCO, 'L'Italia del vino - informazioni, consigli, curiosità e suggestivi itinerari enoturistici', Edagricole, Padova 1994

MAROSO GLORIA, VARANINI GIAN MARIA (a cura di), 'Vite e vino nel Medioevo', Centro di documentazione per la storia della Valpolicella, Verona 1984

MORGANTI PAOLO, SANDRO SANGIORGI, 'L'Amarone della Valpolicella', Morganti editori, Sona (Verona) 2003

MORGANTI PAOLO, TONELLI LETIZIA, 'Scoprire la val d'Orcia', Morganti editori, Sona (Verona) 2003

MONTORI MARCO, PELLEGRINI FABIO, 'Viaggio a piedi dalle crete senesi a Montalcino alla val d'Orcia', Editrice grafica l'Etruria, Cortona (Arezzo), 1989

POLINI DAVIDE, 'I luoghi del gusto', Baldini & Castoldi, ottobre 2000

PELLUCCI EMANUELE, 'Il Brunello di Montalcino, un vino, una storia', stampato in proprio dall'autore, Fiesole (Firenze) 1986

PELLUCCI EMANUELE, 'Il Brunello e gli altri vini di Montalcino', Vipsul edizioni, Firenze 1999

PETRINI CARLO, 'Città del vino', Civin srl, Siena 2001

PICCINARDI ANTONIO, 'Dizionario dei vini italiani', Biblioteca Universale Rizzoli, Milano 1991

RAFFAELLI ILIO, 'Prima dell'economia del Brunello - Montalcino: urbanistica, demografia, cultura e società, dalle origini ai nostri giorni', Le Balze, Montepulciano (Siena) 2001

RAFFAELLI ILIO, 'Un pioniere del vino Brunello: Riccardo Paccagnini', Type Service editore, Montalcino (Siena) 1990

RAFFAELLI ILIO, 'Creatività popolare montalcinese', Nencini editore, Siena 1996

REDI FRANCESCO, 'Bacco in Toscana', Veronelli editore, Bergamo 1995

THOMASES DANIEL, 'Vini in Toscana', Edizioni Demomedia, Firenze 1999

TULIANI MAURIZIO, 'La tavola imbandita - note su alimentazione e società a Siena nel Medioevo', Betti editrice, Siena 2001

VEZZOSI ALESSANDRO, 'Il vino di Leonardo', Morgana edizioni, Firenze 1991

ZANFI ANDREA, 'Andar per tavola in Toscana, guida enogastronomica', Alsaba edizioni srl, Siena 2001

ZOI PIERO, 'Il Moscadello di Montalcino - un vino, un paese, una storia', Panozzo editore, Rimini 1993

photographic and illustrative contributions

The photographs in this book are the property of 'Morganti editori', who have acquired the rights. In relation to the norms on author's rights, the following is a list of photographers' names (the numbers correspond to the numbers on the illustrations).

- **Alexander Brookshaw**: 1-2-3-4-6-7-8-9-10-11-12-13-14-15-16-18-19-20-21-22-23-29-42-43-44-45-46-49-51-53-55-56-58-59-60-61-65-67-68-69-71-72-73-74-77-78-79-80-81-82-83-87-89-90-91-92-93-94-95-96-99-100-101-103-104-108-109-112-118-119-121-122-124-125-126-127-128-130-132-138-139-140-142-143-146-148-150-151-152-155-157-159-160-161-162-164-165-166-167-168-169-170-171-172-173-174-175-177-178-179-180-181-182-183-184-185-186-187-189-190-191-192-193-194-195-196-197-198-199-200-201-202-203-204-205-208-209-210-211-212-213-214-215-217-218-219-220-222-224-227-228-229-230-231-233-234-235-236-237-238-239-240-242-244-245-246-247-248-249-250-255-258-259-260-261-262-263-264-265-266-267-268-269-270-271-272-273-274-275-276-277-279-280-281-282-283-284-285-286-287-288-289-290-306-307-308-309-310-311-312-313-314-315-316-317-318-319-320-322-323 (also some of the photographs of the bottles and producers)
- **Sandra Raccanello**: 5-17-24-25-28-30-41-47-54-57-62-64-70-86-106-110-111-113-114-116-129-137-141-145-156-158-163-176-188-206-207-221-225-243-251-252-293 (also some of the photographs of the producers)
- **Fernando Zanetti**: 63-66-97-107-115-120-133-144-147
- **Carlo Cipriani**: 153-223-241
- **Alessandra Garusi**: 148-232
- **Stefano Gaspari**: 98-123-131-134-216-226 (also some of the photographs of the bottles)

Some of the photographs in the book have been supplied by companies that, declaring themselves owners of the rights of use and also in agreement with their photographers, have authorised anonymous reproduction (without author's name). The cellar brands have been supplied by same. The texts relative to the companies have been published only after agreement and authorisation of interested parties. Some photographs have been provided by the following archives:

- **archivio Nettari di Bacco**: 26-27-76-253
- **archivio Banfi**: 294-295-296-297-298-299-300-301-302-303-304-305
- **archivio Tenuta Greppo di Franco Biondi Santi**: 135
- **archivio azienda agricola Brandi** (photos di Paolo Busato): 254-256-257
- **archivio Raffaelli**: 50
- **archivio Tenuta Col d'Orcia**: 75-102-105
- **archivio Museo della comunità di Montalcino e del Brunello**: 291-292
- **archivio Tenuta di Argiano**: 126
- the animal illustratios (caption numbers 31-32-33-34-35-36-37-38-39-40-321) were realised by **Mariano Caminoli**

A note of thanks:

- **Museo civico e diocesano d'arte sacra** of Montalcino for the permission granted to photograph several pieces of their collection (authorisation 1 december 2002)
- **Enzo Tiezzi** for his kind openness in granting us the possibility to photograph his collection of archeological artifacts (photos 43-45-46-46)

contents

Summary 7

1. A WINE OF SUCCESS 8

2. THE TERRITORY 18
    THE TYPICAL FLORA 27

3. THE HISTORY OF BRUNELLO 30
    From the origins to the middle ages 32
    Towards Brunello 37
    Biondi Santi and Brunello..43
    From the flask to the Bordeaux bottle 47

4. UNDER THE SIGN OF SANGIOVESE 52

5. FROM VINEYARD TO CELLAR 62
    From the vineyard to the wine cellar 69
    The rules of production 73
    The slopes 77
    Aging 78
    The riserve 84
    The old vintages 87
    New and old cellars..90
    The future of *futures*...93
    Where is Brunello going? 95

6. THE OTHER WINES OF MONTALCINO 98
    Moscadello di Montalcino 100
    Sant'Antimo..105
    Rosso di Montalcino..110
    Vin Santo..115

8. **THE LAND OF BRUNELLO** 118
THE TERRITORY OF MONTALCINO 121
Montalcino..123
CIVIC AND DIOCESE MUSEUM OF SACRED ART 132
Castelnuovo dell'Abate 136
THE ABBACY SANT'ANTIMO 138
Sant'Angelo in Colle 142
Camigliano...144
Torrenieri...145
Parishes and castles 147

9. **TYPICAL PRODUCTS AND CUISINE**....................150
Ilcinese cuisine 152
Extra virgin olive oil 154
The honey..157
The cheeses...158
The curing of pork...160
Sienese Crete truffles 164
The pinci..165
Taglioli al Brunello 166
Sweets and pastry 167
Wild game 168
Brunello grappa 169
Orcia Valley saffron 170
Banfi balsamic production 173
Pinci with Brunello ragout sauce 174
Rice with red chicory, Pecorino and Brunello 176
Duck with Brunello Grappa 178
Old style 'peposo'..180
Veal titbits with Brunello 182
Rabbit with Brunello...184
Fillet of Chianina covered with Brunello
on Zolfini beans..186
Breast of Hen-Pheasant with Brunello 188

10. **MUSEUM AND FOLKLORE**...190
The promotional activities of Brunello....................192
THE STARS OF BRUNELLO 194
The Museum of the Community of Montalcino
and Brunello..196
The museum of glass 197
MUSEUM OF GLASS...198
The feast of the thrush 200

FIGURES AT THE FEAST OF THE THRUSH.............................202
The other feasts..205

11. THE PRODUCERS 206
Altesino 208
Argiano..210
Banfi 212
Biondi Santi 214
Bolsignano 216
Castello Romitorio 218
Casisano Colombaio..220
Castello Romitorio 222
Ciacci Piccolomini d'Aragona.................................224
Col d'Orcia 226
Corte Pavone 228
Costanti 230
Donatella Cinelli Colombini 232
Fanti tenuta san Filippo 234
Fattoria dei Barbi..236
Gorelli le Potazzine 238
Lambardi...240
la Magia 242
le Macioche...244
il Marroneto..246
Mastrojanni 248
Palagetto...250
Paradiso..252
la Pescaia 254
Pian dell'Orino..256
Pian di Macina 258
Poggiolo 260
il Poggione 262
Tiezzi 264
la Torre...266
Uccelliera 268
Villa le Prata...270

Other producer of Brunello di Montalcino 270
A gastronomical tour of the land of Brunello 274
Bibliography 279
Photographic and illustrative contributions............282
Contents 283

OTHER TITLES IN THE SERIES

EDITORIAL COORDINATION
Stefania Conte

ART DIRECTOR
Meri Salvadori

EDITING OF THE ITALIAN TEXTS
Maria Letizia Tonelli

EDITING OF THE GERMAN TEXTS
Carmen Ohlmes

TRANSLATION OF THE GERMAN TEXTS
Verona Business (Petra Feinaigle)

TRANSLATION OF THE ENGLISH TEXTS
Verona Business (Edward Pruett) and David Vance

Printed in Italy

Morganti editori sas
via Morino, 5 - 37060 Sona (Verona)
telephone +39 045 6081114 and +39 045 6089739
fax +39 045 6089739
E-MAIL: morgantieditori@morgantieditori.it

ISBN: 88-87549-27-3

The book has been completed on the 15th of October 2003.
Possible changes, relative to tables, e mail addresses,
internet sites, telephone numbers, prices, products, or other that are subsequently verified after the above date
or in any case not noted in writing, are not the responsibility of Morganti editori.
We shall, however, be happy to insert possible corrections and additions in the subsequent edition.

This volume was printed in the month of November 2003,
with the types of Morganti editori of Sona (Verona).
The paper utilised for this publication is entirely opaque 135 g GardaMatt Art
and glossy opaque 170 g GardaMatt Art for the cover jacket.
The characters employed are Democratica, **Frutiger**, New Baskerville, Optima e Zapf Dingbats